YOUR *Best Life* NOW

STUDY GUIDE

YOUR
Best Life
NOW

STUDY GUIDE

7 STEPS TO LIVING AT YOUR FULL POTENTIAL

JOEL OSTEEN

WARNER
Faith®

New York   Boston   Nashville

Scriptures noted NIV are taken from the HOLY BIBLE: NEW INTERNATIONAL VERSION®. Copyright © 1973, 1978, 1984 by International Bible Society. Used by permission of Zondervan Publishing House. All rights reserved.

Scriptures noted NKJV are taken from the NEW KING JAMES VERSION. Copyright © 1979, 1980, 1982, Thomas Nelson, Inc., Publishers.

Warner Faith
Time Warner Book Group
1271 Avenue of the Americas, New York, NY 10020
Visit our website at www.twbookmark.com

The Warner Faith name and logo are registered trademarks of the Time Warner Book Group.
Printed in the United States of America
First Warner Faith printing: September 2005
10   9   8   7   6   5   4   3   2   1

ISBN: 0-446-69636-6
LCCN: 2005926408

CONTENTS

CHAPTER I

ENLARGING YOUR VISION

FOR MANY OF US, *SOMEDAY* MARKS THAT IMAGINARY MOMENT WHEN WE WILL SOMEHOW get a better life, recover perfect health, and magically break free from crushing debt.

We hope that special *someday* comes, but something deep inside us knows that *someday* won't come by accident or by wishing it were so.

Changed outcomes demand changed thinking. As I mentioned in the Introduction of *Your Best Life Now*:

> "*Today is the only day we have.* We can't do anything about the past, and we don't know what the future holds. But we can live at our full potential right now" (p. x, emphasis added)!

I. Describe your first reaction to the above statement. Did something inside you recoil from it or immediately agree with it? Why?

_____

_____

_____

_____

_____

I

Read what Jesus and the Apostle Paul said below, and then review the statement from the Introduction above:

> "Therefore *do not worry about tomorrow*, for tomorrow will worry about its own things. Sufficient for the day is its own trouble" (Matthew 6:34 NKJV, emphasis added).

> "Brethren, I do not count myself to have apprehended; but one thing I do, forgetting those things which are behind and *reaching forward to those things which are ahead*, I press toward the goal for the prize of the upward call of God in Christ Jesus" (Philippians 3:13–14 NKJV, emphasis added).

2. NOW, how do you feel about the statement quoted from the Introduction?

_____

_____

_____

_____

_____

Some people might believe these two scriptures disagree over how we should treat the future. I believe they actually work together to stress the importance of realizing the future's potential, and emphasizing the positive power of acting today.

3. Discuss or explain how you reach forward to things ahead without worrying about the future.

   HINT: You put your trust in _____ and "reach forward toward things ahead" by living "at your full _____ right _____ !"

_____

_____

_____

_____

If you have trouble conceiving things on the inside, then you probably have trouble receiving on the outside.

4. Take a moment to examine your thought life. Is there some barrier in your mind that produces wrong thinking? What do you think is blocking you from God's best (p. 3)?

_____

_____

_____

_____

_____

_____

_____

> "As long as you can't imagine it, as long as you can't see it, then it is not going to happen for you."
>
> *(p. 3)*

5. Write out five negative phrases you've said that began with the words "I'll never . . ." Describe how those statements could potentially limit your life in some way if left unaddressed.

_____

_____

_____

_____

_____

6. Have you ever known someone who envisioned success in ways that resemble Tara Holland's story (p. 45)? What did you honestly think of that person at the time? Did you find it easy or difficult to support their dream? How do you envision your own success?

_____

_____

_____

_____

_____

_____

7. How do you see yourself most of the time—are you "messing up" and failing, or are you living out a dream and achieving goals? Explain why.

_____

_____

_____

_____

_____

8. Small-minded thinking and God's immeasurable favor do not mix. Reflect on the following questions:

- What if you were offered the chance to race through your favorite store and keep everything you could collect in 15 minutes? What kind of container would you look for? Why?

_____

_____

_____

_____

_____

- Think of your favorite sports figures or dramatic performers. Now imagine them taking your mind-set onto the playing field or performance stage. Would this athlete be able to complete the passes, cross the goal line, or make the final three-point shot before the buzzer? Or, would they be overwhelmed by the pressure? Would that performer boldly deliver their lines and complete complex dance numbers, or become paralyzed with the fear of failure and humiliation? How would your type of attitudes and thinking affect their performance?

HOW BIG IS YOUR BLESSING CONTAINER?

The prophet Elisha gave a curious command to a woman facing traumatic debt problems in 2 Kings 4:1–7. God offered her immeasurable favor, but she had to find containers big enough to hold God's blessing.

What parallels can you draw between her situation and the problem you are facing today?

The prophet told this wife and mother that God would multiply the little bit of oil she had. Then he said, "Go, borrow vessels from everywhere, from all your neighbors; empty vessels; *do not gather just a few*" (2 Kings 4:3b NKJV, emphasis added). She and her son gathered every jar and container in the village and they were all filled.

The supernatural supply ended when the woman's capacity to contain it ended. God's source of supply is immeasurable. How big is your blessing container? What can you do to help increase your capacity?

Jesus said you can't "put new wine into old wineskins" (see Matthew 9:17). God is looking for a human being to contain the new wine of His Spirit, love, grace, and blessing . . . What would new "wineskins" look like in your life?

9. Answer the following questions by circling the words that best describe you:

- Are you soft or hard?
- Are you pliable or unbending?
- Do you stretch when under pressure, or do you feel ready to explode?
- Is your thinking dominated by faith or by fear?

- Which do you think about more: *God's greatness* or *your weakness*?

——————————————————

_____

_____

_____

_____

_____

_____

_____

_____

_____

_____

_____

_____

_____

_____

"The good news is, God wants to show you His incredible favor. He wants to fill your life with new wine, but are you willing to get rid of your old wineskins? Will you start thinking bigger? Will you enlarge your vision and get rid of those old negative mind-sets that hold you back?"

(p. 6)

10. What is your dream or vision? Is it founded on God's abundance and does it line up with God's Word? Take time to reflect on the following questions prayerfully:

- Have you released it to grow and has it come to pass?
- Or, do you keep it hidden under a cloud of doubt based on thoughts of lack, limitation, and fear of the unknown?

_____

_____

_____

_____

_____

_____

11. If you read about my wife, Victoria, and her vision for a new home (and my doubt-filled response to it), then you know I finally came around and linked my faith with hers. Together, we did three things that might help you. Find them on page 8 *in the book*, list them, and describe or discuss how they may apply to your life and the lives of others close to you:

We kept on . . .

     a. _____ it

     b. _____ it

     c. _____ it

GOD IS TRYING TO PLANT NEW SEEDS IN YOUR HEART!

God says, "See, I am doing a new thing! . . . Do you not perceive it?"
(Isaiah 43:19 NIV)
"Everything is possible for him who believes."
(Mark 9:23 NIV)

I had learned to handle large visions differently by the time God planted a vision in me for moving the Lakewood Church congregation into the Compaq Center:

> ". . . This time, I expanded my vision. I let the seed take root. I conceived it on the inside. I began to 'see' our congregation worshiping God in the Compaq Center in the heart of Houston" (p. 11).

12. What are *you* doing differently now? How can you allow God's seed of vision to survive in your heart? How can you avoid smothering it with doubt, fear, and unbelief?

_____

_____

_____

_____

_____

13. Think about the difference in thinking between the King of Saudi Arabia and the famous golfer on pages 11–12. The king's response demonstrated thinking on a larger scale. How are you thinking right now? What are some attitudes you could change that would enlarge your vision?

_____

_____

_____

_____

_____

God wants to bless you, so don't limit Him with small thinking. Enlarge your vision and release Him to bless you with a God-sized blessing that brings Him glory!

CHAPTER 2

RAISING YOUR LEVEL OF EXPECTANCY

WHEN YOU WERE A TODDLER, THREE STEPS FORWARD WITHOUT A FALL PRODUCED STANDING ovations and thrilled approval from everyone important to you. It took a little more to earn applause when you reached the age of six, and a lot more by the time you hit twenty.

You know you are maturing when you set goals and expectations for yourself instead of relying on the performance standards of others. Growth *should* produce higher expectations.

If your expectations this year are the same as they were last year or ten years ago, then you may be trapped in a "life rut"—a life track or path of living that resembles a grave with two open ends.

> "Now faith is the substance of things hoped for, the evidence of things not seen."
>
> *Hebrews 11:1 NKJV*

The Apostle Paul said, "When I was a child, I spoke as a child, I understood as a child, I thought as a child; but when I became a man, I put away childish things" (1 Corinthians 13:11 NKJV).

God is trying to plant some new seeds in your life, so He wants to see some raised expectations on your behalf. Don't be rocked to sleep by monotony—if you are not going forward in some way, then you are going backward.

This is why I recommend that you "start your day with faith and expectancy, and then go out anticipating good things" (p. 13).

1. How do you usually start your day?

_____

_____

_____

_____

_____

2. Reflect on what you think about the most. Do you approach each day and situation with the glass-half-empty viewpoint, assuming and expecting the worst? Or, are you generally a glass-half-full person who assumes and expects the best?

_____

_____

_____

_____

_____

_____

_____

3. Where have you been asking God to meet you? (It is usually a place that matches your level of expectancy.) Does He routinely go to the preschool to find you? Or, do you often meet Him in the college of faith and hope (even though you may feel very low)?

NOTE: God is _willing_ to descend to the very gates of Hell to meet you when necessary, but He wants you to grow beyond the ABC's of faith and raise your expectations to match His unending faithfulness (see Hebrews 6:1–3).

"God usually meets us at our level of expectancy. If you don't develop the habit of expecting good things to come your way, then you're not likely to receive anything good. If you don't expect things to get better, they probably won't."

(p. 14)

_____

_____

_____

_____

_____

_____

_____

_____

_____

_____

_____

_____

_____

_____

_____

_____

_____

_____

_____

_____

_____

God: "Where shall I meet you?"

You and I: "Can You come down low where I am?"

God: "I have already gone to the bottom for you so that you may come up higher where I am. I have reserved a seat for you in heavenly places . . . if you can break through your fear of heights."

(Ephesians 2:4–7)

4. Do the following statements sound like you? If you've said it, thought it, or lived by it, then *circle it*. (Don't be embarrassed — most of us must plead guilty to one or most of these.)

- "It just isn't fair!"
- "Why me? What did I do to deserve this?"
- "More bad news. So what else is new?"
- "If I didn't have bad luck, I wouldn't have any luck at all."
- "I'm so poor that I can't even pay attention."

- "I'm so busy with my troubles that I wouldn't even notice if any good things came along."
- "I'm too overwhelmed to hope for something better."
- "Nothing good ever happens to me, and I doubt if it ever will."
- Fill in the blank: _____

_____

_____

_____

_____

_____

5. Now explain or discuss the comments you circled in light of these two statements from page 14:

- Our expectations set the boundaries for our lives.
- You have what your faith expects.

_____

_____

_____

_____

_____

6. Seven times in the Scripture, God asks, "What do you see?" (see p. 18). Let me ask you the same question right now. What do you see? Are your eyes focused on your failures and fears, or is your vision filled with the possibilities and super ability of God? Explain your answer below or discuss it with others.

_____

_____

_____

_____

_____

7. Read Psalm 1, keeping your friends and family in mind. Think about the people in your life who know your dreams for the future, and reflect on the following questions:

- Do they usually encourage your dreams?
- Do they often discourage you or talk about your silliness or impracticality?
- Do they consistently draw you closer to God and a godly life?
- Do they share your deepest values and life purpose, or do they scoff at such things?

_____

_____

_____

_____

_____

_____

Find a safe place to dream. Associate with people who inspire you to dream bigger, climb higher, and raise your expectations. Each day:

- See yourself receiving good things.
- Expect the favor of God.
- Expect His blessings.
- Expect to increase.
- Expect promotion.
- Get up and face each day with enthusiasm, knowing that God has great things in store for you.
- Keep your mind set in the right direction—no matter what.

_____

_____

_____

_____

_____

_____

_____

Make a copy of this list, and use it in your personal devotions, in discussions with others, and in your daily work.

CHAPTER 3

———— ❦ ————

GOD HAS MORE IN STORE!

EVERY TIME I THINK ABOUT TODD JACOBS AND THE OPPORTUNITY HE MISSED BECAUSE OF fear, I am reminded of the danger of growing accustomed to the status quo (p. 21). It is easier to live life with a false sense of security, trusting in an unfulfilling job to provide security for our families. But in reality, only God's plan for us can offer true security.

How disappointing it would be to hear the Apostle Paul rewrite his celebrated declaration of the high calling in Christ in Philippians 3:13–14 to say:

> "Brethren, I am not interested in apprehending anything; the only thing I do is focus on those things which are behind. I carefully avoid looking forward to those things which are ahead, settling for nothing more than the goal of getting by, leaving the risky struggle for some pie-in-the-sky prize of the upward call to others."

NOTE: This is NOT Holy Scripture! It is, however, an accurate reflection of the negative way many of us approach the Christian life.

I. How did you feel in your spirit as you read this negative rewrite of Paul's anointed words? Explain why you felt this.

_____

_____

_____

_____

_____

2. What do you do when you find yourself thinking like this negative example of Paul's words?

Take a moment to read the correct version and let it speak to your spirit:

"Brethren, I do not count myself to have apprehended; but one thing I do, forgetting those things which are behind and reaching forward to those things which are ahead, I press toward the goal for the prize of the upward call of God in Christ Jesus" (Philippians 3:13–14, NKJV).

_____   ———— ❧ ————

_____

_____   God has more in
                                 store, but what you
_____   will receive is
                                 directly connected to
_____   how you believe.

_____   *(p. 22)*

_____   _____

_____

_____

_____

_____

3. Ask yourself, "Am I limiting God with inflexible thinking or low expectations concerning my job, my finances, my family relationships, or my involvement in the church and personal ministry? Am I thinking big enough?" Write down and discuss your answers with someone you trust.

_____

I shared with you how my father beat the odds and broke the curse of poverty that overshadowed his family for generations (pp. 25–26). One of the greatest life lessons I learned from Daddy was he refused to limit God. He stayed focused on the dream. He didn't want to leave his family a legacy of mediocrity. Are you *the latest victim* in a long line of family members struggling with poverty and low expectations? Perhaps you struggle with a physical limitation, racial prejudice, or personal sorrows. Are you prepared to declare to your situation, "Enough is enough!" and make the appropriate changes in your life?

4. Take a moment and describe the mountain you are facing.

Then make this declaration over your life and the situations you face: "Armed with the promises of God and the power of the cross of Jesus, I will break the curse over my life and my family. But it will surely come, 'Not by might, nor by power, but by my Spirit, saith the LORD of hosts' " (Zechariah 4:6b).

5. What things in your life seem impossible to overcome at the moment? Take a moment to pray about your fears, asking God for His help.

_____

_____

Perhaps your situation more closely resembles mine, where your parents or grandparents broke a curse of poverty, bondage, or physical disease over your family and pioneered a new future through their faith, determination, and hard work. That means you have been handed a legacy—it is *your* turn to take what you have been given and *multiply and expand* it for the generation after you!

Declare these words over your life:

> "Through the power of God and armed with His Word, I will be a good steward of the gift given to me. I will sow it in faith and expect a great harvest in my lifetime and in the lives of the generations that will follow me. In the name of Jesus and through His ability, I pray. Amen."

6. List some ways you can become a better steward of the gifts and talents God has given you. Identify some of the obstacles in your life that tempt you to settle for mediocrity.

_____

_____

_____

_____

_____

_____

Jesus told His disciples that they would do greater works than He did. John 14:12 says, "Most assuredly, I say to you, he who believes in Me, the works that I do he will do also; and greater works than these he will do, because I go to My Father. And whatever you ask in My name, that I will do, that the Father may be glorified in the Son. If you ask anything in My name, I will do it." That is quite a statement, but is the heart of God. We have a God that wants each generation to experience progress.

7. What are some steps you can take this week to move toward your God-given destiny? What prayers have you been holding back from God because you've been afraid to ask Him?

_____

_____

_____

_____

_____

_____

_____

_____

_____

_____

8. How do you think God might use you to affect future generations?

_____

_____

_____

_____

_____

_____

_____

Post this thought in a place where you see it each morning before you start your day:

I will affect generations to come with the decisions that I make today.

CHAPTER 4

BREAKING THE BARRIERS OF THE PAST

SOMETIMES PEOPLE AND GENERATIONS WHO PIONEERED BREAKTHROUGHS IN THE PAST become the greatest opponents of pioneering breakthroughs today. As humans, we have a tendency to hold down everyone and everything else to just *below* the level of our *own* highest achievement.

Sports stars set records in one decade and desperately hope no one in the next generation can surpass the records they set while in their prime.

Surgeons who pioneer surgical techniques may find it difficult to accept newer techniques developed by others that are safer and more efficient.

A drug company invests millions to develop a breakthrough drug, and ten years later desperately opposes the introduction of a new and better drug developed by another company.

1. How would you describe yourself: a settler, resisting change and struggling to accept new things; or a pioneer, putting forth effort, striving to take risks? Why?

_____

_____

_____

_____

_____

_____

2. In any case, you face barriers in your life that seem to limit your advancement or progress. What are they?

_____

_____

_____

_____

_____

3. Describe the dreams, goals, or tasks you feel God has planted in your life, whether or not you feel you have pursued them.

_____

_____

_____

_____

_____

4. What are some of the hard choices you face with these dreams, goals, or tasks? What are the risks you face when challenging the barriers in your life?

_____

_____

_____

_____

_____

As I noted in *Your Best Life Now*, a *stronghold* is "a thinking pattern that keeps us imprisoned in defeat" (p. 30). Roger Bannister had to break through several strongholds in his day to break the four-minute-mile barrier. For example, most of the experts in middle-distance running were more interested in maintaining the four-minute barrier than in helping anyone actually break through it.

BANNISTER BROKE THE BARRIER OF THE MIND

When Roger Bannister broke the four-minute-mile barrier, he was a full-time medical student. He had no free time to train for the mile run, so he carefully planned out his lunch break and trained for only thirty minutes at a time, three or four times per week. He tapped his medical training to devise controversial new athletic training techniques that are still used today.

When Bannister finally broke through the impossible four-minute barrier, he did it on a day that was so windy that officials nearly called off the attempt. Despite the obstacles on May 6, 1954, Roger Bannister became the first man to break the four-minute-mile barrier with a time of 3:59.4.

In recent times, *Sports Illustrated* rated Bannister's breakthrough as the most significant athletic feat of the 20th century (shared with the first ascent of Mount Everest). Bannister, who came from a poor working-class family, also managed to complete his medical training and become one of England's most prestigious neurologists and researchers. Dr. Bannister was awarded knighthood in 1975 for his medical contributions.

The same may be true of the experts in your life. If the counsel does not come from the Word of God or is primarily rooted in doubt and unbelief, seek out a higher quality of counsel.

God created you to overcome challenges using the principles of success in His Word. Make God's Word your first and most important source of advice in every area of life.

5. Describe some of the "expert counsel" you have heard that protected some artificial barrier better than it equipped you for a breakthrough.

The Hebrews wandered in the wilderness needlessly for forty years after they failed the test of faith at the edge of their promise. Many people fail a grade in school and are forced to remain behind a whole year until they can pass the grade.

6. Are you being tested at the edge of a promise in your life? Explain your situation—what factors in your attitude will determine whether you are going to pass the grade or be held behind.

_____

_____

_____

_____

_____

7. Is there something in your past that endangers your future? Describe or discuss it in detail, along with your plans to press through that barrier. Don't rush through the thinking process on this question. It may be one of the most important things you do this year—for yourself and for those who follow after you (see p. 31)!

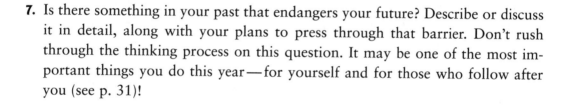

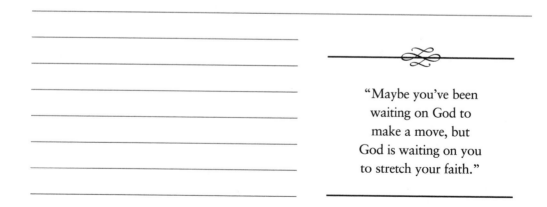

"Maybe you've been waiting on God to make a move, but God is waiting on you to stretch your faith."

8. Oftentimes, sin is passed down from generation to generation. Failure often begets more failure, and success tends to beget more success. What are you producing in your life? Why (see p. 34)?

_____

_____

_____

_____

_____

My final word to you for this chapter is taken from pages 35 and 36. I'm launching it toward you in the same way I would throw a life preserver to someone in danger of drowning. If you are doing fine, then give it to a friend, relative, or enemy who needs it. This is *real help* deeply rooted in the principles of God's Word:

> Break through those barriers of the past. This is a new day, and God wants you to do a new thing. Enlarge your vision. Stretch your faith. You can be the first. You can be the one to "raise the bar." If you believe, all things are possible, then make up your mind that you are going to be the one to set the new standard.

9. Did you sense something stirring deep inside you when you read the words printed above? What are you going to do about them now?

_____

_____

_____

_____

_____

CHAPTER 5

INCREASING IN FAVOR

THE CONCEPT OF *FAVOR* MAY BE HARDER FOR US TO ACCEPT THAN ALMOST ANY OTHER Bible principle. Western society and culture seem to measure worth by what we do, where we come from, how much money we have, or the outward success we've achieved.

The truth is that even our salvation isn't based on what we do, where we come from, or how hard we try to be good. Salvation is God's gift to us through Jesus, His Son. We can't earn it, nor do we deserve it. It is the highest form of favor that God extends to us.

Because we are children of God we are a favored people. The Bible clearly states, "God has crowned us with glory and honor" (Psalm 8:5). Favor means "to assist, to provide with special advantages and to receive preferential treatment" (p. 38). But tragically, many people who accept God's gift of salvation actually live as if God's favor ended the day they were saved. But that is not what God's Word teaches!

1. Read Psalm 8:5, which says God has crowned us with "favor and glory." Do you feel like "God's favor surrounds you like a shield"? Explain.

_____

_____

_____

_____

_____

_____

Reread the following passage from page 39:

> My attitude is: I'm a child of the Most High God. My Father created the whole universe. He has crowned me with favor; therefore, I can expect preferential treatment. I can expect people to go out of their way to want to help me.
>
> Please don't misinterpret what I'm saying. In no way should we ever be arrogant, thinking that we are better than somebody else, that everybody owes us a living or ought to bow down to us. But as God's children we can live with confidence and boldness, expecting good things. We can expect preferential treatment, not because of *who* we are, but because of *whose* we are. We can expect people to want to help us because of who our Father is."

2. Why do you think some Christians are reluctant to expect preferential treatment from God? From others?

_____

_____

_____

_____

_____

3. Describe instances in your own life when you sensed God's favor upon you. Did you feel you deserved it, or was it obvious to you that the favor was a free gift from God?

_____

_____

_____

_____

Let me encourage you to start expecting and declaring God's favor in your life. Every morning before you leave the house, say something like this:

"Father, I thank You that I have Your favor. Your favor is opening a door of opportunity. Your favor is bringing success into my life. Your favor is causing people to want to help me."

Make a point to realize you have the favor of God. Learn to declare it!

4. What steps can you take to declare and experience God's favor in your life (see p. 41)?

_____

_____

_____

_____

_____

5. How do you normally respond when you feel like God is not granting you favor?

_____

_____

_____

_____

_____

God is not some cosmic slot machine dispensing prizes for lucky gamblers who somehow hit the right combination. His love for us is constant and unchanging, and so are the promises in His Word.

However, any visible evidence of God's favor for us personally may be temporarily delayed for a greater good that we cannot see.

For example, Daniel the prophet prayed for divine revelation concerning the end times, and God heard the prayer instantly. The Bible says the delivery of God's answer was delayed for twenty-one days due to cosmic warfare in the heavenly realm (see Daniel 10:12–13). As I wrote on page 43:

> "But just because I didn't get what I wanted doesn't mean that I'm going to quit believing in the favor of God. No, I know God has my best interests at heart, that He is working everything for my good. A delay may spare me from an accident. Or a delay may cause me to bump into somebody that needs to be encouraged, somebody that needs to see a smile. No matter what does or doesn't happen, keep believing in the favor of God in your life."

6. Describe an incident in your life that may have been the unseen favor of God at work in your life. Then, think about a situation where a delay actually worked for your good or preserved your safety.

Take a moment to offer a prayer of thanks to God for working out all things for good in your life, meditating on Romans 8:28:

> "And we know that all things work together for good to those who love God, to those who are the called according to His purpose" (NKJV).

CHAPTER 6

―――――――――――――⚬⚬⚬――――――――――――――

LIVING FAVOR-MINDED

How do you experience God's favor in everyday life? How do you recognize and expect favor in the ordinary details of daily routine? Is it possible to live favor-minded when the days of the calendar seem to blur from week to week and month to month?

It all begins as we believe and live by God's promises:

> "The steps of a good man are ordered by the Lord, and He delights in his way" (Psalm 37:23 NKJV).

You can count on this hardworking promise day by day and step by step. It helps explain how God assists you, provides special advantages, and arranges preferential treatment for you at unexpected times in surprising ways!

We should thank God for the big miracles and acts of favor He gives us, but we should also learn to recognize how He invades our routines and daily duties with countless gifts of favor. God is at work all around us if we take time to prayerfully open our eyes (see p. 44). His favor is something we should never take for granted.

1. Describe how His favor recently affected the ordinary details of your life.

―――

―――

―――

_____

_____

_____

When you live favor-minded, God's blessings will chase you down and overtake you! Do you find that hard to believe? It is in the Bible! Read Deuteronomy 28:1–13 and Galatians 3:13–14.

2. Explain how these promises of God apply to your life right now.

_____

_____

_____

_____

_____

3. How do favor-minded people increase the level of favor in their daily lives? Do you feel like you have been limiting the favor God wants to give to you? Why or why not (see p. 46)?

_____

_____

_____

_____

_____

4. If you can't imagine God ever wanting to bless you, will God's favor "chase you down and overtake you"? Why (see pp. 48–49)?

_____

_____

_____

_____

_____

_____

_____

God's favor is vital if you want to be productive and fulfill His purposes for your life. Perhaps you have lost heart because you made a mistake, or you feel you failed God in some way. Take your cue from the real people in the Bible who fell, blew it, missed it, lost it, and dropped the ball. Remember that Jesus was the One perfect person in all of history.

5. Pick one of the people from the Bible mentioned in this chapter and describe why you relate to his or her situation. (See pp. 48–50 for character sketches on King David, Noah, Ruth, Joseph, and Job.)

_____

_____

_____

_____

_____

6. What have you learned from these biblical examples to help you start living a favor-minded life?

_____

_____

_____

_____

_____

_____

_____

_____

"Friend, if you can learn to stay in an attitude of faith, and in your darkest hour boldly declare the favor of God, then nothing is going to be able to keep you down."

(pp. 50–51)

Did you notice that each of these Bible standouts needed faith to see God's favor turn their lives around? Favor doesn't just happen. If you want to experience God's favor, then first you must live with an attitude of faith. Favor won't happen unless you change your thinking, live by faith, and become favor-minded.

Never underestimate the power of God's favor. One touch of His favor can turn everything around!

7. One of the most useful questions used to help people shatter mental limitations and small-thinking prison cells goes like this:

   "If you had all of the money and resources needed, and you were offered the opportunity to do anything you've dreamed of doing all of your life, what would you do?"

   Do you realize that is exactly what God is offering you in His Word? Now, what will you do about it?

   _____

   _____

   _____

   _____

   _____

   _____

When you read about our desire to purchase a valuable TV time slot for our ministry (pp. 51–52), did you notice that things didn't happen quickly? It didn't just happen after we prayed and made our first request of the network. We had to declare God's favor day after day, while month after month passed by with no change in our circumstances.

There were times earlier in my life when I would have given up too soon, but God helped me learn from my mistakes and I grew in faith. It took more than eight months to see God's favor come to pass, but we stood our ground in prayer and declared God's favor by faith.

Do you want to live a favor-minded life and enjoy God's blessings? Then *never give up on God*. The Bible says, "If you will hope to the end, divine favor will come" (see 1 Peter 1:13).

8. Review this checklist below drawn from page 52, and mark the items you already practice by faith. Think how each of these benefits of understanding God's favor can transform your life and the lives of others:

- Living with confidence comes easy now.
- I dare to be bold.
- I will ask for things I don't normally ask for.
- I view my adversaries in a new way.
- Deep down inside I know I have an advantage in life.
- I've got an edge.
- I have the favor of God!

CHAPTER 7

❧

WHO DO YOU THINK YOU ARE?

UNDER THE BEST CONDITIONS, WE FIRST BEGIN TO DISCOVER WHO WE ARE AS BABIES, SUR-rounded by unconditional love and approval from parents, relatives, and neighbors. This may have helped us form a strong self-image that carried us through the battlefields of sibling rivalry, schoolyard playgrounds, and adolescence.

Did you launch into life from the positive springboard of a loving family or struggle through the destructive environment of a dysfunctional childhood? In any case, your self-image is central to everything you will do and accomplish in life.

I. The Bible says, "For as [a man] thinks in his heart, so is he" (Proverbs 23:7a NKJV). How does this verse relate to the statement quoted above?

_____

_____

_____

_____

_____

_____

_____

❧

"The truth is, you will never rise above the image you have of yourself in your own mind."

(p. 56)

_____

_____

2. What do you think about yourself? Do you think it differs from how God sees you?

_____

_____

_____

_____

_____

3. Read Matthew 12:34–35. Describe your gut reaction to this statement: "The reason your self-concept is so important is: You will probably speak, act, and react as the person you think you are." How does this principle apply to the way you feel about yourself in your heart?

_____

_____

_____

_____

_____

4. Write down the phrases that dominate your conversations about yourself or list some of your personal attributes. Then answer and explain these self-evaluation questions:

- Do you downgrade yourself in front of other people?
- Do you brag about yourself and then laugh nervously?
- Do you say negative things about your past track record?
- Do you predict that unfortunate or negative things will happen to you?
- Do you complain when good things happen to other people, resenting that they don't happen to you?

_____

_____

_____

_____

_____

The Bible says God "declares the end from the beginning" (see Isaiah 46:10). In other words, He declares things even before they exist!

When God looks at you, He sees the finished product, His completed work and wonder of grace in your life. We see it in His treatment of unlikely heroes and reluctant leaders such as Moses and Gideon (see Exodus 3, 4; and Judges 6, 7).

Neither of these men thought he amounted to much, and both tried to talk God out of His crazy idea that they were leaders. They didn't understand that God often speaks into existence what isn't visible in His leaders at first.

The best way to change the image you have of yourself is by agreeing with God. Start seeing yourself as God sees you (see p. 59).

5. How do you think that is done? Are you doing it now?

_____

_____

_____

_____

_____

6. Consider for a moment about how you think and talk about yourself. Do you usually focus on your weaknesses or on God's strengths?

_____

_____

_____

_____

7. Describe how you feel about the statement "God only chooses imperfect people." Do you realize that these are the only candidates God has available to Him? Why do many people seem prone to thinking others are more qualified?

_____

_____

_____

_____

_____

8. Poor self-image is like a communicable disease—it can infect others. Describe ways or incidents in which you were infected or affected by other people with low self-esteem.

_____

_____

_____

_____

_____

9. I described the children of Israel who died in the wilderness this way: "Their lack of faith and their lack of self-esteem robbed them of the fruitful future God had in store for them" (p. 61). _Is it possible_ that a lack of faith and poor self-esteem is attempting a robbery in your life? Explain your answer.

_____

_____

_____

_____

_____

10. Read page 62 and fill in the blanks below. The odd fact about the incident with the children of Israel in the wilderness is this:

God had already _____ the Hebrews the _____, but because of their poor _____-_____, they never made it into the Promised Land. They never fulfilled their _____, all because of the _____ they _____ themselves.

Look closely at the words you put in the blanks. This fill-in-the-blank exercise was included for a very purposeful reason—you face the same situation today! Jesus Christ personally guaranteed you victory. All of God's promises are yours. Victory is yours right now, even if you must wait in faith for it to appear!

_____

_____

_____

_____

_____

11. How do you see yourself right now in the light of what you have learned thus far?

_____

_____

_____

_____

_____

There is only one cure for the *grasshopper mentality* syndrome. Learn to see yourself as God sees you! Choose not to focus on past failures, defeat, and self-pity (pp. 62–63).

12. Where do you turn to learn how God sees you? Write down your answer, and consider some of these ideas as well:

• See how He treats children, women, and men throughout the Scriptures.

- Notice the ways He developed and worked with His flawed leaders from Genesis to Revelation.
- Watch how Jesus patiently worked with men and women having widely different attitudes, personalities, abilities, and training. In the end, He turned the world upside down with His band of unlikely leaders.
- Track God's patient preparation, restoration, and installation of Saul, who became Paul the apostle (see the Book of Acts, chapter 9).
- See what God says about you and anyone else who comes to Christ in repentance and surrender.

_____

_____

_____

_____

_____

In other words, reprogram your mind with God's Word!

13. As a final step for this chapter, join me as we follow in my daddy's footsteps and get a vision of who we are in God's sight. Lift up your Bible and say aloud with me, "This is my Bible. I am what it says I am. I have what it says I have! I do what it tells me to do. I believe what it says is true."

_____

_____

_____

_____

_____

_____

CHAPTER 8

~~~

UNDERSTANDING YOUR VALUE

WHERE DOES YOUR VALUE COME FROM? THE BIBLE SAYS GOD CREATED US IN *HIS IMAGE* and *according to His likeness* (Genesis 1:26–27). That means He embedded an image of Himself inside you. And now He wants to see you bloom!

During the Depression era, a short, scrubby-looking racehorse with the hidden heart of a champion was regularly losing races. Everyone who was anyone in the racing circuit had labeled this low performer as a loser.

Then a new and inexperienced owner bought Seabiscuit, hired a washed-up trainer and a jockey with a bad reputation to work with him. They discovered that if they broke with standard racing style and forced Seabiscuit to lie back and look directly into the eyes of his toughest competitor, then Seabiscuit would do what it took to win!

Seabiscuit defied the experts of the day, and his surprising string of dramatic wins captured the attention of a nation struggling to arise from the Depression. Seabiscuit even overcame a career-ending injury to soundly defeat the top-rated racing horse of that era to transform horseracing history.

No one understood the value of Seabiscuit for years. The heart of a champion was embedded in the body of an unattractive horse that everyone regarded as a loser. Once someone discovered and released Seabiscuit's hidden strength and value, the champion on the inside broke the stereotypes to write a new chapter in the world of horseracing.

1. Do you feel there is a champion living on the inside of you?

_____

_____

_____

_____

_____

_____

Your value is intrinsic; it was part of you before you were born (p. 67). You were made in the image of God, and that eternal part of your soul longs for and steers you toward destiny.

2. Have you ever felt a sense of destiny for your life? Explain your answer.

_____

_____

_____

_____

_____

_____

The greatest measure of your value is the price God paid to save you. The Bible says:

> "For God so loved the world that *He gave His only begotten Son*, that whoever believes in Him should not perish but have everlasting life. For God did not send His Son into the world to condemn the world, but that the world through Him might be saved" (John 3:16–17 NKJV, emphasis added).

3. If God gauges your worth by the magnitude of His love for you, then how should you measure your own worth?

_____

_____

_____

_____

_____

_____

For some reason, we often feel we must be perfect to receive love and respect from other people and from God. The Bible pops that perfection bubble without question: "For all have sinned and fall short of the glory of God" (Romans 3:23 NKJV). You aren't perfect, but you are a work in progress (p. 67).

4. Read this promise from the Bible and explain what it might mean for your life:

"Being confident of this very thing, that He who has begun a *good* work in you *will complete it* until the day of Jesus Christ" (Philippians 1:6 NKJV, emphasis added).

The young man named Steve who suffered from severe rejection (see p. 69) felt guilt over being born. Perhaps you feel the same way Steve did, or you know what it is like to live or work in a negative environment subjecting you to constant criticism and humiliation. I told Steve, "Don't allow the rejection of other people to cause you to reject yourself."

_____

_____

_____

_____

5. Genesis 1:26 tells us that all of humanity was created in God's image. We all bear the image of God, whether we acknowledge this fact or not. Check the things you do personally to remember your true image in Christ, and describe the results in your life:

- I let every form of misinformation or hurtful communication go in one ear and out the other.
- I constantly remind myself that I am made in the image of Almighty God.
- I remind myself that He has crowned me with glory and honor, and that I am God's own masterpiece.
- I refuse to let other people play games with my mind.
- I don't let others deceive me into thinking that my value has diminished.

_____

_____

_____

_____

_____

_____

6. In the last paragraph of chapter 8 of *Your Best Life Now*, I wrote, "No matter what you go through in life, no matter how many disappointments you suffer, your value in God's eyes always remains the same." Jesus made a promise to you. Describe how it affects your sense of value:

For He Himself has said, "I will never leave you nor forsake you." So we may boldly say: "The LORD is my helper; I will not fear. What can man do to me" (Hebrews 13:5b NKJV)?

_____

_____

_____

_____

_____

_____

_____

_____

CHAPTER 9

BECOME WHAT YOU BELIEVE

Many people roll their eyes in disbelief whenever someone talks about "receiving what you believe." They scoff at the idea that their words or negative thinking patterns have any power to affect their lives.

1. What went through your mind when you read the story about Nick, the railroad crewman who froze to death in an abandoned refrigerator car that was only slightly cooler than normal room temperature?

_____

_____

_____

_____

_____

_____

> "We don't always get what we deserve in life, but we usually get no more than we expect; we receive what we believe."
>
> *(p. 72)*

2. Have you heard the confession of Job, the man who suffered so much in the Old Testament? He said, "For *the thing I greatly feared* has come upon me, and *what I dreaded* has happened to me" (Job 3:25 NKJV, emphasis added). Describe times when this was true in your life or in the lives of people you know.

_____

_____

_____

_____

_____

_____

When Jesus talked about the end times, He included the words "fear" and "expectation":

"... men's hearts failing them from fear and the expectation of those things which are coming on the earth, for the powers of heaven will be shaken" (Luke 21:26 NKJV).

3. Do you think this implies that Jesus scoffs at the power of fear and expectation? Why or why not?

_____

_____

_____

_____

_____

_____

God wants you to win the battle of your own mind (p. 73). The battle turns in your favor as you learn to believe for good things, especially the things God says about you and the promises He makes to you. The Bible says:

"Yet in _all_ these things _we are more than conquerors_ through Him who loved us. For I am persuaded that neither death nor life, nor angels nor principalities nor powers, nor things present nor things to come, nor height nor depth, nor any other created thing, shall be able to separate us from the love of God which is in Christ Jesus our Lord" (Romans 8:37–39 NKJV, emphasis added).

4. What would it take for you to be *persuaded* in the same way as the Apostle Paul? God's Word says, ". . . in *all* these things you can be more than a conqueror."

_____

_____

_____

_____

_____

Jesus told the two blind men, "According to your faith be it done unto you" (see Matthew 9:29–30, p. 75). It was their believing that brought them the healing.

5. Answer the following questions:

- Who or what do you depend upon in times of trial or crisis?
- These men *believed* God and *received* from God. Where do you fit into this pattern?
- Are you a believing receiver yet?

"What *you* believe has a much greater impact on your life than what anybody else believes."

(p. 75)

_____

_____

_____

_____

_____

6. Read the two questions Jesus asked His disciples in Matthew 16:13–15. Why do you think Jesus went on to ask the second question? (**HINT:** Reread the quote above.)

_____

_____

_____

_____

_____

7. Read Matthew 16:16–19 and think about Jesus' reaction to Peter's declaration of personal belief. If Jesus asked you the same question, what would you say? Are you building your life around your firm belief that Jesus is your Savior?

_____

_____

_____

_____

_____

8. If you become what you believe, in what ways and areas would you begin to believe for greater things? Why?

_____

_____

_____

_____

_____

God always finishes what He begins, and He always does things well (p. 78). *The Message* translates Philippians 1:6: "There has never been the slightest doubt in my mind that the God who started the great work in you would keep at it and bring it to a flourishing finish on the very day Christ Jesus appears." You may say you believe that, but how can you show that it applies to you and your life?

9. Describe how the promise of Philippians 1:6 holds promise for you each day.

_____

_____

_____

_____

_____

_____

_____

10. How do you handle tough times and conflict (see pp. 78–79)?

Describe some of the choices you have made that seem to line up with the Bible.

_____

_____

_____

_____

_____

Describe the actions you take and choices you make in tough times that you know aren't biblical or good for your well-being. What can you do to change your actions?

_____

_____

_____

_____

_____

11. Choose the statement below that best describes how you live your life right now. Describe or discuss your choice and how it is lived out in your life (p. 79):

- I need to see it to believe it.
- I need to believe it to see it.

_____

_____

_____

_____

_____

12. God made a tremendous promise to Abraham and Sarah. But it didn't come to pass for about twenty years because, in my opinion, Sarah first had to conceive the promise of a son in her heart before she could conceive in her aged body. Jesus made you a promise too: "I want you to live life to the full, till it over-flows" (p. 80).

Do you think God is waiting for you to conceive the promise in your heart? Explain your answer.

_____

_____

_____

_____

_____

How will you change your thinking to conceive and receive what Jesus promised you?

_____

_____

_____

_____

_____

CHAPTER 10

DEVELOPING A PROSPEROUS MIND-SET

SADLY, I AM CONVINCED THAT A VERY LARGE NUMBER OF THE PEOPLE WHO ATTEND church services weekly and call themselves Christians are like the naive traveler described at the beginning of this chapter. Remember how this man didn't realize he could partake in fine dining on the cruise ship? In the same way, God's people are missing out on the blessings He freely gives, because we don't realize that the good things in life have already been paid for. As we travel on our way to heaven, we often don't realize what has been included in the price of our ticket God purchased for us.

Naive spiritual pilgrims have all of the privileges of royalty as the King's kids, but they go through life living on cheese and crackers outside of God's banquet hall. They lie awake night after night on the ship of life, wishing they could be free from the endless cycles of fear, poverty, and the dreariness of third-class citizenship.

They are family! It is time to step up and feast at God's dining table!

1. Disappointments and setbacks often cause us to dig out the stale cheese and crackers again (p. 85). Are you in a feast or a famine at the moment? Explain your answer.

_____

_____

_____

_____

_____

Too many of us give up at the first sign of failure. When we get knocked down by adversity, failure, or fear, we are tempted to stay down. The Bible says, "A righteous man may fall seven times and rise again" (Proverbs 24:16). No matter how much you failed or missed it in the past, you have a bright future if you put your life totally in God's hands. Get a fresh vision of what God can do in your life and develop a prosperous mind-set (p. 85). If one dream dies, don't be afraid to dream another dream!

2. What do you believe God can do in your life?

_____

_____

_____

_____

_____

3. Now for a harder question: What do you think God *wants* to do in your life? What are you doing to cooperate with God?

_____

_____

_____

_____

_____

4. A deeply embedded poverty mind-set can rob you of God's best (p. 86). What do you see yourself doing, receiving, and becoming in the next year? The next five years? Have you made some goals?

_____

_____

_____

_____

_____

5. Does your vision speak of poverty and lack, or is it a testimony to God's prosperity and the abundant life?

_____

_____

_____

_____

_____

Read about King David's kindness toward Mephibosheth in 2 Samuel 9:1–13. Jonathan and David had a covenant relationship with one another. They were best friends. Whatever one had, also belonged to the other. If Jonathan needed food or money, he knew he could go to David's house and get whatever he needed. They mutually felt obligated to take care of the other's family, should something happen.

David found himself in a position to help Jonathan's son, Mephibosheth. Knowing that David was an enemy of his grandfather Saul, Mephibosheth feared David when he called for him. Jonathan's son had been living in a poverty-stricken city for almost his entire life. He did not expect David to bless him with kindness.

6. Do you see yourself as God's champion, or are you like Mephibosheth, who saw himself as a defeated loser, a dead dog (p. 87–89)? Why?

_____

_____

_____

_____

_____

Guilt burdens some people so deeply that they feel they aren't good enough to worship God with other worshipers. For these people, going to church dredges up feelings of unworthiness and memories of past failures. It is hard for them even to walk into a worship service. Others have left the old life behind. They joyfully enter into praise and worship, and eagerly look forward to new opportunities to serve, minister, and engage in fellowship with other people.

Imagine if you were a parent, but had children who did not trust you to provide their daily needs. What if you found out one of your sons was saving scraps from every meal under the bed, fearing you would not attend to the daily needs of the family. First of all, you would probably feel horrible that your own son would worry about such things. You *might* also feel like he didn't trust you to be a good parent.

God is saying to His children that He is worthy of our trust and He has prepared a banquet table for us to feast on in this life just because we are kids of the King. And, the great news is there is plenty to go around!

7. Where are you right now? Are you reaching for another lonely round of cheese and crackers, or are you ready to rise up and go to the banquet hall?

_____

_____

_____

_____

_____

8. List some qualities that come to mind when you think of royalty. What kind of life should a child of a King live?

_____

_____

_____

_____

_____

_____

_____

_____

_____

_____

"Well done, good
and faithful servant;
you were faithful
over a few things, I
will make you ruler
over many things.
Enter into the joy of
your lord."

(Matthew 25:21b NKJV)

CHAPTER 11

─────────❧─────────

BE HAPPY WITH WHO YOU ARE

DO YOU AVOID MIRRORS AND LARGE STORE WINDOWS? DO YOU SMIRK OR FEEL UNEASY when someone shows your photo or video image? Does the sight of someone aiming a camera at you spark anger or resentment? Do you find yourself wishing you were someone else?

1. Do you like yourself? Why?

_____

_____

_____

_____

_____

_____

_____

_____

─────────❧─────────

According to Jesus,
the second great
commandment is
this: "You shall love
your neighbor *as
yourself.*"

*(Matthew 22:39 NKJV,
emphasis added)*

2. It is hard to love other people if you don't love yourself. Do you feel as if you are at the mercy of everyone else around you when it comes to approval and self-esteem?

_____

_____

_____

_____

_____

_____

No one really wants to admit they are insecure in some way, but since the goal of this study guide is to help you _live your best life now_, honesty is a necessity—even if it hurts. If you are like me, then you have caught yourself living to please other people instead of being true to God and yourself (p. 91).

3. Think of some ways you have lived to please other people in the past. How did it affect your relationships?

_____

_____

_____

_____

_____

What things can you change in your life to live as an original, not a copycat (p. 92)?

_____

_____

_____

_____

_____

4. Describe in fifty words or less "the person God made me to be." Share it with a family member or a person in your discussion group who knows you well. Ask them if, in their opinion, your description is accurate.

_____

_____

_____

_____

_____

AN ACCURATE PICTURE OF THE REAL YOU

For You formed my inward parts; You covered me in my mother's womb. I will praise You, for I am fearfully and wonderfully made; marvelous are Your works, and that my soul knows very well. My frame was not hidden from You, when I was made in secret, and skillfully wrought in the lowest parts of the earth. Your eyes saw my substance, being yet unformed. And in Your book they all were written, the days fashioned for me, when as yet there were none of them (Psalm 139:13–16 NKJV).

---

5. Copies come from molds. Originals are handcrafted, one-of-a-kind works of creative art. Which word describes the way you see yourself: copy or original?

_____

_____

_____

_____

6. If God handcrafted you, then is it even possible for you to be a mistake or an error of God? Why do you think it is so easy to forget our worth in today's culture?

_____

_____

_____

_____

_____

_____

_____

_____

_____

_____

_____

_____

_____

_____

_____

_____

_____

_____

_____

> "It's okay to be you!
> God made you the
> way you are on
> purpose. He went to
> great lengths to
> make sure that each
> of us is an original.
> We should not feel
> bad because our
> personality, tastes,
> hobbies, or even
> spiritual tendencies
> are not the same as
> another person's."
>
> *(p. 92)*

7. Describe some of the problems you encountered after you compared yourself to other people (on page 94, I described how I went on a guilt trip after comparing my prayer life to that of another minister on television).

_____

_____

_____

_____

_____

8. The Bible commands each of us to "examine his own work" (p. 95). Take a moment to examine your life — but don't do it by comparing yourself to other people. Use God's Word and the things He has revealed to you as your measure of

true success. Write down the things you learn from the process. Are you doing some things God never assigned you to or equipped you to do? Remember: Not all "good" things are "God things."

_____

_____

_____

_____

_____

9. Describe some of the people who come to you for advice and counsel. What fruit can you see in their lives from your counsel? How much of your counsel has been based on the principles or examples in the Bible?

_____

_____

_____

_____

_____

10. Who do you go to for advice? How does their counsel produce fruit in your life?

_____

_____

_____

_____

_____

11. The proverbial cow leans against the fence in chest-high green grass thinking, "The grass is always greener on the other side of the fence." What a waste of energy and resources! Now for a potentially painful question: Do you find yourself still wanting to be something or somebody you are not?

_____

_____

_____

_____

_____

_____

12. Reflect on some of the ways the biblical principles in this chapter have helped you with the greener grass problem, or how they provided you with knowledge to help others battling this problem.

_____

_____

_____

_____

_____

_____

Moses tried to fulfill his destiny on his own and failed as a young man. God gave him a second chance and Moses confronted Pharaoh and led the children of Israel out of Egypt at the age of 80. Peter stuck his foot in his mouth countless times and publicly denied Jesus three times; but he got up, repented, and issued the first salvation call in the early church.

God built value into us when He created us (p. 67). Jesus lived this out during His earthly ministry. Again and again, He broke cultural and religious taboos to touch and heal lepers, minister to tax collectors (social and political traitors), and eat with such sinners as prostitutes.

One of His last conversations on the cross was with a convicted thief, to whom He offered eternal life! God doesn't expect us to come to Him perfect. If we were perfect, then Jesus would have never come. Jesus said, "A physician doesn't come to the healthy, it is to the sick that I am sent."

CHAPTER 12

CHOOSING THE RIGHT THOUGHTS

SEVERAL YEARS AGO A PAIR OF MOVIES HIT THE BIG SCREEN FEATURING A LOVABLE, WISE-cracking robot as the central star and hero figure. One word seems to define this robot in the minds of many who remember the movie: Input!

This mechanical marvel with a human personality was starved for "input" to feed its vast memory banks and satisfy its craving for knowledge.

Your mind far surpasses the complexity of the finest computer systems man can make. It is the ultimate multitasker and creative interpreter of data, working around the clock from its earliest moments of existence until its final function at death. The continuous service life of the human computer may span as much as one hundred years or more!

At least two things are significantly different about your brain—*you* decide what input goes in and when, and where to focus your virtually unlimited thinking power.

Some people focus the potential of their incredible brains on advanced theories of astrophysics, while others prefer to memorize endless columns of sports statistics. A few study the intricacies of human languages while entire generations prefer to focus on the latest fashions, street slang, and social trends.

> If you want to live at your full potential, then you must discover the power of your thoughts and words.
>
> *(p. 101)*

1. Thoughts determine _____ , _____ , and
   _____ - _____ (see p. 101).

   _____

   _____

   _____

   _____

   _____

2. Almost like a magnet, we _____ _____ what we constantly think
   about. And our _____ also affect our emotions. We will feel exactly
   the _____ we _____ (see p. 101).

   _____

   _____

   _____   ⸙

   _____   "Nobody can make
                                    us think about
   _____   something. God
                                    won't do it, and the
   _____   enemy *can't* do it.
                                    You decide what you
   _____   will entertain in
                                        your mind."
   _____
                                   (p. 102, emphasis added)
   _____

   _____

   _____

   _____

3. In a society seemingly addicted to the blame game, God wants each of us to accept responsibility for our own choices. *Describe* a time in your life when the
   enemy planted a negative, discouraging thought in your mind and you chose to
   water it, nurture it, coddle it, and help it to grow (p. 102).

_____

_____

_____

_____

_____

4. Describe your first reaction to this statement: "If you are depressed, you must understand, nobody is *making* you depressed. If you're not happy, nobody is forcing you to be unhappy. If you're negative and you have a bad attitude, nobody's coercing you to be bored, uncooperative, sarcastic, or sullen."

_____

_____

_____

_____

_____

5. Below are some statements you read on page 103 in *Your Best Life Now*. Did you find that your thoughts and feelings changed when you read these statements?

- Actually, your circumstances don't have you down. Your *thoughts* about your circumstances have you down.
- It's time to think about what you are thinking about.
- Obviously, we can't ignore problems and live in denial, pretending that nothing bad ever happens to us. That is unrealistic.
- Focus your thoughts on the One who has promised, "Those who wait on the Lord shall renew their strength."

_____

_____

_____

_____

_____

_____

_____

_____

_____

_____

_____

> "When you think positive, excellent thoughts, you will be propelled toward greatness."
>
> *(p. 104)*

6. Are you entirely happy about where your thoughts are propelling you?

_____

_____

_____

_____

_____

_____

_____

7. Read Philippians 4:8. List the higher things and positive things of God in Philippians 4:8.

_____

_____

_____

_____

_____

_____

Identify the things on that list that dominate your thinking, those that only cross your mind occasionally, and those that never seem to find their way into your mind.

Finally, honestly confess the times you have focused on things that opposed this list in God's Word.

Negativity, cynicism, scorn, and pessimism are viruses and diseases to the human soul. They eat away at your personality and faith like runaway cancerous growths. If they dominate your thoughts, they will dominate your life (p. 107).

The negative farmer in my story was so dominated by negativity that he wouldn't change his attitude even when faced with a miracle! It *is* possible for you to re-dig the riverbed of your life, but it is a process Paul described as "being transformed by the renewing of your mind" (p. 108). It does not happen instantly. You do it thought by thought, word by word, and decision by decision.

This transformation process involves *correcting* wrong thoughts or vain imaginings and *investing* in godly thoughts (p. 109). Godly thoughts are based upon God's Word.

8. Write down key Scripture passages that have influenced your life.

_____

_____

_____

_____

_____

9. Make note of the Scriptures or the biblical principles mentioned in *Your Best Life Now* that really captured your attention and why.

_____

_____

_____

_____

_____

Do you still find it hard to believe God has confidence in you? Remember that Jesus placed the future of the Church in the hands of twelve very ordinary men, along with Paul who distinguished himself as the greatest enemy of the Church in its early days. If you can catch a glimpse of how much confidence God has in you, you will never again shrink back into an inferiority complex (p. 110).

I've described to you how God used my wife, Victoria, to encourage me and believe in me when I doubted myself. It was because of her faith in God and her confidence in me that we are on television and serve as pastors for such a wonderful church today.

10. Do you have anyone who has faith in God and is also confident in you? Describe and discuss their effect on your life. If there is no one like this in your life, ask God to send you a friend, a prayer partner, or a leader in your church to help you fulfill your God-given destiny and purpose.

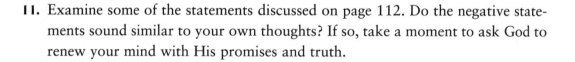

11. Examine some of the statements discussed on page 112. Do the negative statements sound similar to your own thoughts? If so, take a moment to ask God to renew your mind with His promises and truth.

CHAPTER 13

REPROGRAMMING YOUR MENTAL COMPUTER

GIGO IS ONE OF THE BEST-KNOWN COMPUTER TERMS DATING BACK TO THE BEGINNING of the digital age. This four-letter acronym stands for "Garbage In, Garbage Out." When you were born, your computer-like mind was essentially a blank page, a clean hard drive ready for programming.

A lot has happened in this technological age since you were born, but the quality and content of your thinking still depends upon the quality and content of what you feed into your mental computer.

With all of the wrong thinking, incorrect information, and painful memories we store in the caverns of our minds, it is easy to be negative. Sometimes you simply have to choose to see the bright side of situations (p. 113).

1. Describe and discuss difficult situations in which you wanted to camp around the bad news, but you chose to see the bright side and made the best of it. What might have happened if you had gone the other way?

2. Reread the story about the lonely man who thought he had emotional problems, but in reality was dealing with thinking problems (pp. 114–115). Based on what you've read so far, explain why you do or do not have thinking problems.

_____

_____

_____

_____

_____

3. Do you agree with these statements taken from page 115? Comment on each statement below.

- God made you, and He has programmed you for victory.
- Our emotions simply respond to what we're thinking about.
- Our emotions allow us to feel what we're thinking.
- You have to reprogram your mental computer, and when you do, your emotions will follow.

The Bible says, "I have set before you life and death, blessings and curses, positive and negative; therefore God says choose life."

(see p. 115)

_____

_____

_____

_____

_____

_____

4. Did God say He would *make* choices for you? Does He sometimes *advise* you about choices?

_____

_____

_____

_____

_____

_____

5. Think about some of the choices you've made recently, and whether those choices brought you a taste of life or a taste of death, a blessing or a curse, positive or negative results.

_____

_____

_____

_____

_____

_____

6. What ran through your mind when you read this statement: "We never get to a place where we don't have to deal with negative, destructive thoughts" (p. 116). What emotions did you feel?

_____

_____

_____

_____

_____

_____

In this chapter I confessed my thoughts of failure when I was going through the trial of relocating Lakewood Church. I said, "It's impossible. It's never going to work out" (p. 117). Were you surprised that I would share the negative thoughts I had during a severe attack of discouragement? Why do you think I shared this? (**HINT:** Who is better qualified to talk with you about discouragement—someone who has really *struggled* with discouragement *and even failed at times* before winning the battle, or someone who hasn't really faced those problems?)

7. How would this principle apply to your life?

_____

_____

_____

_____

_____

_____

_____

_____

"When we're always worried, upset, or depressed, all we're really doing is delaying God in bringing the victory. God works where there is an attitude of faith."

(p. 118)

_____

_____

Every minute you allow yourself to lapse into a negative attitude is a minute that God cannot work in that situation (p. 118).

8. Think of a situation in the Bible where negativity, doubt, and unbelief literally limited God. (**HINT:** See Matthew 13:54–58.) Now think of a situation in your own experience when unbelief tied the hands of God.

_____

_____

_____

_____

_____

Many people seem to spend most of their lives on the down side of a hill. They take one step forward only to take two steps backward.

9. Read James 1:6–8, and explain the dangers of vacillating faith and double-minded living.

_____

_____

_____

_____

_____

God brings victory to the consistent. It doesn't matter whether you are physically strong or weak, educated or uneducated, wealthy or working at it. He is looking for people who live out this Scripture passage: "Watch, stand fast in the faith, be brave, be strong. Let all that you do be done with love" (1 Corinthians 16:13–14 NKJV).

10. Describe areas in your life where you need to develop consistency and an unwavering attitude of faith (i.e., faith for the salvation of family members, or for physical healing, or financial breakthrough). Explain how you plan to set your mind for success, victory, and progress (p. 120).

_____

_____

_____

_____

_____

CHAPTER 14

THE POWER IN YOUR WORDS

It shocks me to see how casually we throw around words. According to the Bible, there is power in our words. Yet, a majority of the people might roll their eyes if you say, "We get what we say" (see p. 121). Why should we be surprised by the power of our words when we see how God uses words?

1. Read Genesis 1:3–29; John 1:1–4; and Hebrews 1:2, 11:3. How did Creation come into being according to these verses? List the action words in each of these Scripture passages.

_____

_____

_____

_____

_____

_____

_____

_____

> "Our words have tremendous power, and whether we want to or not, we give life to what we're saying, either good or bad."
>
> *(p. 122)*

2. Explain how words are similar to seeds, and give examples from your own life experience of how this has been true for you (p. 122).

_____

_____

_____

_____

_____

3. We discussed the propelling power of thoughts earlier. But now I want you to answer this question: Where is your tongue taking you (see p. 122, James 3:4–5)? Be honest with yourself when evaluating the fruit of your lips.

_____

_____

_____

_____

_____

4. Jesus met a Roman centurion who had a good grasp of the power of words. Read Matthew 8:5–13 and answer these questions:

- Why was Jesus so amazed by this non-Jewish Roman soldier that He praised him more than anyone in all of Israel?
- What did this soldier say that you could apply to your own life (vs 8)?

_____

"What you say in the midst of your difficulties will have a great impact on how long you stay in those situations."

(p. 123)

_____

_____

_____

_____

_____

One of the slogans issued by the U.S. Government during World War II was: "Loose Lips Sink Ships." It was meant to alert the American people (many of whom were helping to manufacture ammunition, heavy artillery, naval ships, etc.) to the presence of enemy spies who were constantly trying to pick up valuable information about troop movements and military strategies.

5. Explain why that simple slogan might still be true today in our individual lives.

_____

_____

_____

_____

_____

I heard about a man with a serious disease who had nothing to lose, so he began to watch old black-and-white comedy movies that made him laugh. His disease reversed itself and he claimed he had laughed himself back to health!

As a rule, the more positive your thoughts and words, the stronger you will be and the sooner you will get over whatever ails you (p. 123). According to the Bible, the man who said he'd laughed himself back to health may not be so far off.

6. Read Proverbs 15:13, 15; and 17:22. Write some biblical prescriptions for health. How have you applied them to your own life?

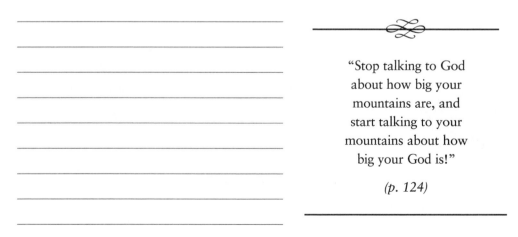

"Stop talking to God about how big your mountains are, and start talking to your mountains about how big your God is!"

(p. 124)

_____

_____

_____

7. There is a miracle in your mouth! Do you know how to release it? Review the story of David's defeat of Goliath (pp. 124–125). Describe some of the keys David used to overcome his "mountain" of an enemy. How did David overcome his mountain of an enemy?

_____

_____

_____

_____

_____

8. Read Mark 11:23. The Bible tells us to speak to our mountains. What mountain are you facing today? Ask God to increase your faith in what He can do.

_____

_____

_____

_____

_____

Learn how to release the miracle in your mouth and watch God turn your situation around!

CHAPTER 15

SPEAKING LIFE-CHANGING WORDS

IMMEDIATELY FOLLOWING MY ACCOUNT OF MOTHER'S MIRACULOUS HEALING OF ADvanced liver cancer, I made a bold statement: "Mother used her words to change her world, and you can do the same thing" (p. 128).

The reason I am so confident is that my statement is based on the supernatural promises of our miracle-working God. It is time that we all learned how to boldly confess God's Word and change our world!

My mother didn't wait for a crisis to confess God's Word. Virtually every day, as long as I can remember, she spoke God's Word over Daddy and over each of us children. She still uses God's Word as a creative force to encourage others and as a spiritual weapon against negativity.

1. How can you affect the lives of your children, family members, or friends by speaking God's Word over them (p. 128)?

_____

_____

"God is a miracle-working God."

(p. 128)

_____

_____

_____

_____

_____

"Your words have enormous creative power. The moment you speak something out, you give birth to it" (p. 129). This is a spiritual principle, and it is true whether we say words that are negative or positive. Words of defeat really do have the power to prevent us from moving ahead in life.

Maybe you feel like there is nothing positive to talk about at the dinner table. You might be thinking, "Joel, you just don't know my situation. It is hopeless." Well, you may be in a very difficult situation, but you could experience a sense of joy in your home if you just began to talk about God's Word at mealtime, instead of complaining. You may be surprised to see how the Lord uses this to change your set of circumstances.

2. Reflect on this statement: "Your words have enormous creative power. The moment you speak something out, you give birth to it" (p. 129). Do you believe this statement? Read Acts 3:1–8 and note the process that takes place from the time a word is spoken to its fulfillment.

_____

_____

_____

_____

_____

3. What do you verbalize or speak most often in your daily routine? Do you feel like you speak more about your "dirty laundry" or about God's promises (p. 129)?

_____

_____

_____

_____

_____

4. Reflect on this statement: "Don't use your words to describe your situation; use your words to *change* your situation" (p. 129). Do you feel like your faith declarations are bold or timid?

_____

_____

_____

_____

_____

I mentioned in chapter 15 that every morning I get out of bed and say, "Father, I thank you that I am strong in the Lord and the power of Your might. I am well able to do what You have called me to do" (p. 129).

It is important that you start your day speaking positive words, starting with God's Word. We need to align our words with His Word. Not only is this a great way to avoid negative talk, but it is a powerful way to unleash God's favor over you and your family.

5. Think for a moment about how you start your day. What are some of your first thoughts as you get out of bed? Write out a prayer that you can say each morning that reflects God's Word. Make a point to declare your prayer boldly each morning.

_____   _____

_____

_____   "Avoiding negative
                                  talk is not
_____   enough . . . You must
                                  get on the offense."
_____
                                  (p. 130)
_____   _____

_____

_____

_____

God has given us hundreds of promises in His Word. Sometimes it is easy to think they are just words that are for our reading pleasure. But they are actually words of life that we should declare boldly, bringing us to victory, hope, and a prosperous future.

6. Read some of God's promises below, then write out some of your favorites from Scripture.

   • "Never will I leave you or forsake you."
   • "I have come so that you might have life abundantly."
   • "I can do all things through Christ who strengthens me."

_____

_____

_____

_____

_____

Sometimes we find ourselves in situations that only God can help us through. This has been true for Victoria and me as we continue to pastor Lakewood Church—we need divine guidance daily. During times of difficult decision-making, we have declared God's promises on wisdom and guidance boldly together. He has always been faithful to show us His way.

7. Are you in a situation that requires an extra measure of wisdom and guidance? Begin to write down passages you find in your daily Bible reading on wisdom and see what the Lord guides you to do in this situation.

_____

_____

_____

_____

_____

CHAPTER 16

<hr>

SPEAKING A BLESSING

IT HAS BEEN SAID THAT WITH GREAT POWER COMES GREAT RESPONSIBILITY. GOD'S WORD puts it this way: "For everyone to whom much is given, from him much will be required; and to whom much has been committed, of him they will ask the more" (Luke 12:48b NKJV).

It should be obvious by this point in our study that we have been given great power with our words. With that power comes great responsibility.

1. God wants us to bless others—Jesus even commanded us to love our enemies and bless those who curse us (Matthew 5:44). This is especially important when we have influence in the lives of other people.

   - List and describe the people whom you influence in some way.
   - Explain how and what you communicate to them.

   _____

   _____

   _____

   _____

   _____

2. Explain some of the dangerous aspects of negative words spoken to others (pp. 133–134). Think about some of your past conversations with a family member

or a friend. What are some of the negative words you shouldn't have said, and would gladly take back if you could? How will the memory of your mistake help you avoid a repeat performance?

_____

_____

_____

_____

_____

3. You read about the importance of a father's blessing to families in Bible times (pp. 133–134). From your reading, explain why we should consider reclaiming the tradition of saying a family blessing over our children.

_____

_____

_____

_____

_____

_____

_____

_____

"Our words affect
our children's future,
for either good or
evil."

(p. 135)

4. Describe what went through your mind when you read the statement "Millions of adults today are still suffering as a result of the negative words their parents spoke over them as a child" (p. 135). Were you thinking about your own painful childhood memories, about harsh words you said to your own children, or perhaps the pain suffered by a close friend?

_____

_____

_____

_____

_____

5. If you are to be the model for your children, then describe what their concept of
God might be (and what you _want_ it to
be).

_____

_____

_____

_____

—————————— ❦ ——————————

"A blessing is not a
blessing until it is
spoken."

_(p. 137)_

—————————————————

_____

_____

_____

6. This question is from page 137 of _Your Best Life Now_: "What are you passing
down to the next generation?" How often do you speak to people younger than
yourself? Do your words and example draw them closer to God?

_____

_____

_____

_____

_____

7. Reread these lines from chapter 16 of the book:

"We need to be extremely careful about what we allow to come out of our
mouths. The next time you're tempted to talk down to somebody, to belit-
tle your child or degrade him, remember: _You can't ever get those words
back_" (p. 138).

_____

_____

_____

_____

_____

8. Examine the most important relationships in your life using these questions:

- Do your most important relationships make you feel valued and accepted or cheap and rejected? Explain.
- Reflect on how you think you make the other members of those relationships feel.
- What do you think is God's best for those relationships?

_____

_____

_____

_____

_____

_____

9. Describe some ways in which you speak and declare blessings over your family and friends, your church, and your own future. Comment on any changes you feel are necessary as a result of studying the biblical truths in this book.

_____

_____

_____

_____

_____

_____

CHAPTER 17

LETTING GO OF EMOTIONAL WOUNDS

THE NEWS ELECTRIFIED VIEWERS AROUND THE WORLD. ONE MAN'S UNSHAKABLE WILL TO survive forced him to make an unthinkable decision. The young man was an expert rock climber who was extremely familiar with the rugged wilderness site he had chosen for what should have been a routine climb. He was well equipped and well trained for the adventure—it was the unexpected that nearly ended his life.

I remember watching television reports and reading detailed accounts of his experience . . . this man was doing everything he had trained to do when suddenly a large boulder shifted, pinning his arm against a rock wall.

He struggled for hours to free his arm, continuously covering different scenarios in his mind of what might happen to him. He was alone. Before long, he knew he had only two choices: give up the struggle and die, or somehow cut off his own arm to free the rest of his body so he could live. The struggle to live was a physical and an emotional struggle. Thoughts of his family and friends flooded his mind as he battled the harsh elements. He knew he wanted to be there for his sister's wedding. He determined in his heart that he would not let her down. He made his decision and acted on it. Devising a makeshift tourniquet, the man slowly amputated his own arm and bandaged the wound. Then he still had to walk for many miles before he reached civilization. All of us face certain decisions in life that seem to reduce everything to two choices: We may choose to cling to something that is dying—and die with it. Or, we may choose to release the thing that is dying in our lives so we can live and start over again.

1. For this reason, the fourth step toward living your best life now is ___ ___ ___ ___ ___ _____ (p. 143).

_____

_____

_____

2. There are two things you must get rid of to be free: a victim mentality and bitterness in your heart.

- What is a victim mentality?
- How have you lived with a victim mentality or experienced this with someone close to you?
- Why must it be removed if you want to live your best life now (p. 144)?

_____

_____

_____

_____

_____

An old vaudeville routine goes, "Doctor, Doctor, my arm hurts when I do *this*. What should I do?" "In my professional opinion, you should stop doing *that*!" Have you ever tried to comfort or counsel friends, relatives, or strangers you met who were more interested in rehearsing their old hurts, woes, and injustices than in receiving fresh hope and assistance? (Keep in mind the fact that very few people are ready for "answers" when hurts, losses, or wounds are *fresh*. This is to be expected and accepted.)

_____

_____

_____

_____

3. Describe situations in your own life or in the lives of people you've known where the attention or sympathy received over a hurt or loss suffered long ago seemed to be more attractive than any solution or help (see the story of "Phil and Judy" on page 145).

"Unless you let go of the old, God will not bring the new."

(p. 146)

_____

_____

_____

_____

_____

"Remember, your emotions follow your thoughts. When you dwell on painful experiences in your past, your emotions go right back there with you, and you feel the pain in the present" (p. 146).

4. Describe a painful memory that recurs in your life, a memory that sometimes reproduces the same emotional pain you felt when it happened long ago.

_____

_____

_____

_____

"Do you want to be made well?"

(p. 148)

_____

5. Do you spend more time citing God's Word over your problem or citing excuses for allowing it to control your life (p. 148)? Why?

_____

_____

_____

_____

_____

6. If you read the story about my mother's childhood bout with polio and her adult battle with cancer, then you also know that she "dug in her heels and fought the good fight of faith" (p. 150). What about you? Do you respond to difficulties and crises in your life with constant complaining or by speaking words of faith and victory? Explain.

_____

_____

_____

_____

_____

7. Are you so driven to understand the *why* behind a crisis or tragedy that you unconsciously put your faith in God on the line for that answer?

_____

_____

_____

_____

_____

- If your answer is YES, then explain what you've learned about the need to trust God first, even when you don't understand.
- If you answered NO, explain how you feel you reached this point in life.

If you really want to get well, you must walk out of any emotional bondage in which you have been living (see p. 152). Describe any emotional bondage in your life, and how you plan to walk out of that bondage using biblical principles.

CHAPTER 18

DON'T LET BITTERNESS TAKE ROOT

IMAGINE BEING LOCKED IN A LARGE BOX IN THE MIDDLE OF A FREE FALL. THERE IS ONE normal person on each side of you along with seven angry people just looking for someplace to explode. You have just imagined yourself taking an average elevator ride on a typical day—where seven of every ten people are angry about something.

It gets worse. Imagine driving on a freeway with nine other cars and drivers. You are in the middle, and seven of the drivers sharing the road with you at that moment are angry about something. In fact, they are human time bombs that could explode in irrational violence at any minute. It seems that this world is becoming the land of the angry.

"A bitter root will produce bitter fruit."

(p. 154)

The problem persists whether you line up ten airline pilots, child-care attendants, schoolteachers, bus drivers, or factory workers. It appears that seven of every ten may have anger issues.

"Before chemical lawn weed control became popular, armies of children were sent on missions to clear front lawns of dandelions, which may well be America's most prolific and unwelcome lawn weed. From block to block across the sodded land, the warning was heard, "Don't just pull off the green leafy tops. You have to go below the surface and get the root or those weeds will come back even worse.

1. Does bitterness, unforgiveness, or unre-solved anger just keep showing up in your life? Describe what you have or haven't done to deal with the root problem be-neath it all.

_____

_____

_____

_____

_____

_____

_____

> "If you have areas in your life where you are constantly struggling, trying to change but finding yourself unable to do so, you need to ask God to show you what's keeping you from being free."
>
> *(p. 155)*

Finding a root of bitterness in the human soul is very similar to searching for buried toxic waste. You look for outward evidence—in this case, negative attitudes, depres-sion, sarcastic words, and uncontrolled anger. Then you trace the infectious toxins or behavior to its source, buried beneath the surface veneer of your life.

2. What do you do with toxic bitterness once you find it in your soul (p. 158)? Ex-plain your answer, using personal examples or experiences if possible.

_____

_____

_____

_____

_____

As you recall my story about the former Methodist minister who was healed of crippling arthritis in his hands (pp. 161–162), consider this promise:

"Trust in the LORD with all your heart and lean not on your own under-standing; in all your ways acknowledge Him, and He will make your paths straight. Do not be wise in your own eyes; fear the LORD and shun evil. This will bring health to your body and *nourishment to your bones*" (Proverbs 3:5–8 NIV, emphasis added).

The Hebrew word translated for nourishment or marrow means "a beverage or moisture"—in other words, refreshment. This minister friend said that once he discovered he was holding onto unforgiveness and resentment toward certain people, he decided to forgive them. One by one, his fingers regained their flexibility until he was totally healed.

One of the first things my mother did when she discovered she had cancer was to examine her life for any signs of bitterness, unforgiveness, or broken relationships (p. 162). This is something all of us should do anyway, but especially when we are battling physical, mental, or spiritual disease.

3. Explain why this process of self-examination is so crucial to maintaining a healthy Christian life.

_____

_____

_____

_____

_____

_____

_____

_____

> "Forgiveness is a choice, but it is not an option."
>
> *(p. 163)*

4. What is *your* choice? Explain ways the truth above applies to areas of your life.

_____

_____

_____

_____

Jesus is the supreme example of what forgiveness looks like. Often, there is a cost involved. Though Jesus was a sinless man, He chose to initiate reconciliation with humanity. He didn't wait for us to come and apologize to Him. In fact, some of His last words were to His Father: "Forgive them, for they do not know what they do."

Our human tendency is to withhold forgiveness if we are the offended person. Yet Jesus did exactly the opposite. Though humanity deserved death, He took our place and suffered unjustly on our behalf. He took on our sin so that we might become the righteousness of God. Now that is radical forgiveness!

5. What are some reasons you have chosen not to forgive a person? Are you waiting on someone to apologize first? How is this severed relationship affecting other relationships?

Jesus said, "If you don't forgive other people, then your Father in heaven is not going to forgive you."

(see Matthew 6:14–14)

_____

_____

_____

_____

_____

_____

_____

6. Take a moment to confess your sins that deal specifically with relationships. Write them down as a prayer. Ask the Lord to restore your broken relationships, and forgive as He has forgiven you.

_____

_____

_____

_____

_____

_____

CHAPTER 19

LET GOD BRING JUSTICE INTO YOUR LIFE

DO YOU TRUST GOD, OR DO YOU SECRETLY FEAR THAT HE REALLY DOESN'T LIKE YOU? Is there a hidden conviction in your mind that God is just too busy to pay attention to the dull details of your life? Even worse, do you think He really doesn't care about what happens to you?

Peter put that lie where it belonged when he said:

> "Humble yourselves therefore under the mighty hand of God, that he may exalt you in due time, casting all your care upon Him; for he careth for you" (1 Peter 5:6–7 NKJV).

John called Jesus our advocate or lawyer. Jesus is pleading your case on your behalf!

Where does that put you now?

1. List some steps you can take to see this happen in your life.

_____

_____

_____

_____

_____

"God is your vindicator. You need to start letting God fight your battles for you. Let God settle your cases."

(p. 164)

91

_____

_____

_____

On page 165 of *Your Best Life Now*, I wrote: "Sometimes God allows us to go through certain things to test us. If you have somebody in your life right now who is not treating you right, that situation may very well be a test of your faith."

If this statement alarms you, then read James 1:13 and notice that I am *not* saying that God tempts us or sends bad things our way. However, the Lord does work through every good and bad thing that comes into our lives, using them to perfect us (see Romans 8:28).

Even Jesus was subject to the school of suffering in preparing for His divine role as Savior. "Though He was a Son, yet He learned obedience by the things which He suffered" (Hebrews 5:8 NKJV). The original meaning of the Greek word *obedience* translates "to hear under . . . or to listen attentively in compliance."[1]

2. Think of difficult experiences that taught you how to listen more attentively for God's voice. Explain why attentive listening is crucial for Christians facing hard times and injustice.

_____

_____

_____

_____

_____

_____

_____

We create some of our biggest problems when we try to help God fulfill a promise through our own manipulation, control, or human intervention (p. 166). The

[1] The overall meaning of the word *obedience* in this Scripture was drawn from the following word definitions from *Strong's*: Greek #5218. *hupakoe*, hoop-ak-o-ay´; from G5219, *hupakouo*.

world is still suffering from the strife produced by Abraham and Sarah's "Ishmael" solution, their human attempt to fulfill God's divine promise (see Genesis 16, 17, 18:1–15; 21:1–20).

3. How have you created an "Ishmael" in your life?

_____

_____

_____

_____

_____

4. Are you being tempted right now to produce an Ishmael out of impatience, frustration, or desperation? Discuss your answer in light of Abraham and Sarah's experience.

_____

_____

_____

_____

_____

5. Review the "To Do" list of recommended positive responses to other people, "no matter how they are treating you" (see p. 167):

- Keep doing the right thing.
- Don't get offended.
- Don't let them get you upset.
- Don't try to pay them back by returning evil for evil.
- Keep extending forgiveness.
- Keep responding in love.

Describe a time when you did these things in an unjust or difficult situation, placing your trust in God.

_____

_____

_____

_____

Describe a time when you did not do these things, and honestly evaluate the consequences that followed.

_____

_____

_____

_____

Even though critics sometimes accuse me of being overly positive, I never present a pie-in-the-sky picture of life. Christians experience hard times, suffering, and discouragement just like everybody else. The difference is that we *know* and *admit* our weakness, and we lean on God's strength and faithfulness in those times. Even so, it is easy to get tired and discouraged when hard times seem to drag on and on.

The Bible says, "Don't get tired of doing what's right for in due season you shall reap if you don't faint" (Galatians 6:9).

6. Answer the following questions and discuss them with your study group or a trusted friend who believes and lives by God's Word.

   • Are you facing a long-term problem that just won't go away overnight?
   • Are you prepared to do the right thing when the wrong thing is happening to you and when change seems to be far away?
   • Are you determined to trust God?

_____

_____

_____

_____

CHAPTER 20

DEFEATING DISAPPOINTMENTS

DISAPPOINTMENT IS AN INTERNAL FORCE THAT CAN LINGER AND OVERSHADOW US 24 hours a day, every day. It is the emotional state we experience when something we expected is less than what we hoped for or—worse yet—doesn't appear at all.

The Bible says, "Hope deferred makes the heart sick" (Proverbs 31:12a NKJV). "Heart sick" seems to say it all. The Bible also says, "The spirit of a man will sustain him in sickness, but *who can bear a broken spirit*?" (Proverbs 18:14 NKJV, emphasis added).

1. "Disappointments almost always accompany setbacks . . . but if you are still grieving and feeling sorrow over a disappointment that took place a year or more ago, something is wrong" (p. 175)!

   • Take a moment to ask yourself, "What setbacks came my way over the last year?" List them and discuss your answer.
   • Now ask yourself: "Am I in some way still grieving or feeling sorrow over any of these setbacks?" Discuss your answer.

   _____

   _____

   _____

If you are still grieving or feeling sorrow over disappointments from the past, then you know something has to change for your own good. You were created to live an abundant life in Jesus Christ, not a sorrowful life locked in the shadow of past disappointment.

2. Read Psalm 31:24 and discuss how you can apply it to your wounds from the past.

_____

_____

_____

_____

_____

_____

Past mistakes can become powerful anchors, binding your soul to the mistakes of yesterday. On page 177, you read about my daddy's dilemma over his failed first marriage: "My dad made a decision that he was not going to allow his past to poison his future."

3. What did he do once that decision was made? (**HINT:** He accepted two things from God.) Have you taken those steps? Explain.

_____

_____

_____

_____

_____

_____

Some disappointments come because of the wrong choices of other people in our lives (pp. 178–179). God will not change another person's will. If your spouse refuses to reconcile, if your boss won't reconsider, if your children refuse to turn around, then you return to your first priority: "But seek first the kingdom of God and His righteousness" (Matthew 6:33a NKJV). Then trust Him for the rest.

4. Describe some ways that your life and future seem to be entangled in the wrong choices or motives of other people. Then reflect on some practical ways you can seek God's kingdom first.

_____

_____

_____

_____

_____

When you focus on things you cannot change rather than on the things you *can* change, you are trying to "put a question mark where God has put a period" (p. 179). Dump that "should have, could have, would have" mentality and realize that God desires your restoration more than you do!

5. Describe some of the "should have, could have, would have" thoughts that tried to dominate your thinking over the last twelve months.

_____

_____

_____

_____

6. How would your thinking change if you based every thought and every word spoken on the deep conviction that God wants you to be restored?

_____

_____

_____

_____

7. The prophet Samuel was deeply disappointed when Saul sinned against God, yet God already had another plan in the wings that was even greater (pp. 180–181). Do you have a disappointment blocking your view of the future? Describe it.

_____

_____

_____

_____

_____

God was already preparing young David's heart as he faithfully kept his father's sheep, even as Saul schemed to steal sheep that God told him to destroy (see 1 Samuel 15). Remember God's goodness in your life, and identify ways that God prepared another plan for your life, even as the first plan for your life seemed to crumble before your eyes.

> "But as it is written,
> Eye hath not seen,
> nor ear heard,
> neither have entered
> into the heart of
> man, the things
> which God hath
> prepared for them
> that love him."
>
> *(1 Corinthians 2:9)*

8. "Faith must always be a present-tense reality, not a distant memory" (p. 184). Disappointments often keep you trapped in the past, where faith is merely something you had or saw working way back when.

   • Describe your faith right *now*. Is it mostly distant memory or present-tense reality? Why?
   • Do you talk more about the good old days or about what you're doing and believing for *today*?

CHAPTER 21

GETTING UP ON THE INSIDE

WHAT EXPERIENCES HAVE MADE THE GREATEST IMPACT ON YOUR LIFE FOR GOOD? MANY times we only discover who we really are after we rise to meet a difficult challenge. James the Apostle said:

> My brethren, count it all joy when you fall into various trials, knowing that the *testing of your faith* produces patience. But let patience have its perfect work, *that you may be perfect and complete*, lacking nothing (James 1:2–4, emphasis added).

1. Few people sharpen their character apart from pressure, difficulty, or failure. Think of a failure that actually produced positive changes in your life, and describe or discuss it in the light of the first chapter of James.

"The fifth step to living at your full potential is finding strength through adversity . . . *we may get knocked down on the outside, but the key to living in victory is to learn how to get up on t he inside.*"

(p. 187, emphasis added)

_____

_____

_____

_____

_____

_____

2. What does God say you should do when you've done everything you know to do in a situation, but it still looks as if nothing is happening (pp. 188–189, see Ephesians 6:13)?

_____

_____

_____

_____

_____

3. Former First Lady Eleanor Roosevelt once said, "No one can make you feel inferior without your consent" (p. 189). As good as that sounds, the Bible says something even better: "Yet in all these things *we are more than conquerors* through Him who loved us" (Romans 8:37 NKJV, emphasis added).

Read the incredible list of things we have conquered in Christ in Romans 8: 35–39. Now add any of your challenges and problems to the list and explain why it is right to do so (surely God is more powerful than your problems).

_____

_____

_____

_____

_____

Defeat often begins with indecision. Make a good decision right now and take your first step away from defeat and toward your next victory! *Choose* to believe God. "You need to change your attitude. You have to get up on the inside. Develop that victor's mentality and watch what God will do" (p. 190).

4. Examine any attitudes that you need to change, and write out one or two key Scriptures that will help you "get up on the inside." How would you describe your mentality over the last six months, based on the things you've read and learned in this chapter of *Your Best Life Now*?

"God wants you to be a winner, not a whiner."

(p. 191)

_____

_____

_____

_____

_____

_____

_____

5. Whining is a mark of immaturity. We expect (but do not accept) whining from toddlers and preschool children, but do *not* expect (nor accept) whining from adults. Why should we expect God to accept such childish behavior (pp. 191–192)?

Do you recall the last time you whined to the Lord about a situation or problem? Give a detailed account of your whining episode. Then make a plan to guard against another episode. List some ways you can intentionally decide to "stand up on the inside."

_____

_____

_____

_____

_____

_____

_____

_____

6. Take a moment to write down the top three problems plaguing your life right now (even if you covered them in previous chapters of the *Your Best Life Now Study Guide*).

Honestly assess whether your problems have you "rolling over like Scooter" or "standing up like David" (see pp. 192–193).

Then write down today's date, place your initials beside it, and pray this prayer:

"God, renew a right, persevering, and steadfast spirit within me. I trust You, and I lean on You with all of my strength and in all of my weakness. Because You live in me, I am full of Your can-do power. I can overcome. I can live in victory. I can stand up on the inside.

"If I get knocked down, I won't stay down. I won't give up; I'll get up. No matter what comes against me in life, I am going to keep standing up on the inside because You live in me!"

CHAPTER 22

TRUSTING GOD'S TIMING

IN THE BATTLE OF TRUST VERSUS FRUSTRATION, WHICH ONE WINS MORE OFTEN IN YOUR life? God promises to cover virtually every area of need or want in our lives, but He is too wise to instantly provide excessively or in lump sums. As with most lottery winners, we would probably watch the blessings run through our fingers and end up as destitute as we were before we met Him. No, God is more interested in building character than in merely filling our bank accounts with money. He *does* bless us with the power to get wealth (Deuteronomy 8:18), but it is only on His terms, on His timetable, and *for His purposes*.

Trust will affect and transform every part of your relationship with God. If you trust God, then you know He often works most when you see it and feel it the least (p. 197).

1. Point out key ways God worked in your life and the lives of others before you became a Christian.

2. Are you frustrated because you don't see God moving in your life right now (p. 198)?

Is it possible that I am praying for things that are not God's best for me (which means His answer to my prayers will probably be different from what I asked for)?

Or, do I sense that the answers to my prayers are being delayed because it is not the right time yet according to God's master timetable?

The Bible says God declares "the end from the beginning" (Isaiah 46:9–10), which means He sees the *whole picture* long before we even realize we are *in* the picture! When we let impatience rule, we become like the novice gardener who planted carrot seeds for the first time. He was so excited about the prospect of seeing carrots grow in his garden that he went out each morning and dug up the seeds expecting to see some early progress toward a harvest.

At first the novice gardener was angry because the carrot seeds didn't produce as advertised. When he asked seasoned gardeners about his crop failure, he quickly learned that his own impatience had killed the seeds before they could germinate and take root. He had learned his first lesson about "due season."

3. Have you been digging up your seeds with the tool of impatience? Remember, "All of the pieces have to come together for it to be God's perfect time" (p. 199).

Think about the three problems you listed earlier, and explain how they are hindering your greatest dream in life.

Now make a list of other pieces to life's puzzle that might not be in place at this time (e.g., people, property, knowledge and skills, favor, governments, spiritual climate, elements of your own character).

_____

_____

_____

_____

_____

_____

_____

_____

_____

_____

> "God already has the answer to your prayers before you have the need. He has already been arranging things in your favor."
>
> *(p. 202)*

4. According to Matthew 6:8, God knows what you need even before you ask Him. When you ask God for things in prayer, what are you *really* wanting Him to do? Circle the answer that best explains your approach to prayer.

   a. I really want to write it down, confess it as done, and let God do it His way while I live life without worry.

   b. I want to ask for it, and continue asking over and over until I feel better.

   c. I'm fighting the strong urge to sit down and map out my own fast-track path to get what I want . . . just to help God out, since He is so busy with so many requests like mine.

d. I just want to give up, because this prayer thing is just too hard and long for me.

_____

_____

_____

_____

_____

5. When my father was struggling to hear God's voice concerning a church building project, he sometimes missed hearing it but he was always honest about his fallibility (see pp. 203–204). What do you do when you feel you missed God's timing in your life or ministry?

_____

_____

_____

_____

_____

CHAPTER 23

THE PURPOSE OF TRIALS

TOUGH TIMES HAPPEN TO EVERYONE. BUT SOMETHING VERY IMPORTANT HAPPENS IN those times: You grow. "If you will learn to cooperate with God and be quick to change and correct the areas that He brings to light, then you'll pass the test and you will be promoted to a new level" (p. 206).

1. Describe the test you are facing at the moment. Where is the greatest pressure for change? Is this the hand of God "bringing light to impurities in your character" (p. 206)?

_____

_____

_____

_____

_____

2. In what way do you believe God is behind it somewhere? How do you think He wants you to respond to this test?

_____

_____

_____

_____

Most of us don't enjoy the process of overcoming difficulty, but we know it is a part of life. Imagine, for a moment, a wrestler who never wrestled against a living opponent, who never lifted weights or trained to increase his strength, and who never bothered to learn any defensive or offensive wrestling techniques. Perhaps an appropriate name for this unfortunate individual would be "Mr. Wimpy."

"It's in the tough times of life that we find out what we're really made of."

(p. 205)

The same scenario applies to would-be Olympic weight lifters who never increase the amount of weight they lift; to figure skaters who never graduate from the simple figure-eight routine; and to would-be physicists or theoretical mathematicians who avoid any difficult problems involving numbers or abstract concepts.

It seems that pressure, applied stress, and systematic movement against resistance, over distance, around obstacles, or through barriers is necessary if you want to experience progress.

3. How is God using people in your life to help perfect your character (pp. 207–208)?

   • What role do these people play in your life? (Be kind!)
   • List some of the things you most dislike about those individuals.
   • Do you think their character flaws may actually be in you? If so, how might God want to change you first?

4. Describe the most trying circumstances you face right now, and how you are praying about them.

_____

_____

_____

_____

_____

5. Now take the time to examine yourself and identify any issues God may be trying to bring to light through these circumstances.

_____

_____

_____

_____

_____

Many people probably wish God would just leave them alone. As far as I can tell, He didn't take a public opinion poll or call for a public vote on His methods and purposes.

The Bible says, "Woe to him who strives with his Maker! . . . Shall the clay say to him who forms it, 'What are you making?' " (Isaiah 45:9 NKJV)

6. The Bible describes us as *clay* in God's hands. What kind of clay do you think you are in His hands at the moment (p. 210)? Soft, pliable, and easily molded; or hard, crusty, and set in your ways? Explain.

_____

_____

_____

_____

7. Is life easy or challenging at the moment? In what ways do you think it is possible to grow in the easier times of life?

"The trial is a test of
your faith, character,
and endurance."

(p. 211)

8. It is easy to think that salvation is a onetime prayer that will make all of life's problems disappear. The Bible, however, reminds us that we are to "work out our salvation" (see Philippians 2:12). On a scale of 1–10, how do you think you are doing with accepting the challenges in your life right now? Pray for God to remove any resentment over the tests of faith you are enduring right now.

CHAPTER 24

TRUSTING GOD WHEN LIFE DOESN'T MAKE SENSE

SOMEONE HAS SAID THE LONGEST AND MOST DIFFICULT JOURNEY OF FAITH IS THE BRIEF passage from the brain to the heart. How many times have you looked into the sky in times of crisis or struggle and said, "Why me, Lord? Why now? Why here?" Those of us who haven't said it have to admit we've thought it a few times.

Everyone tends to reach a point in their season of suffering when they will have some questions about what is happening. When Daddy had to deal with the pain and uncertain future created by my sister's birth injuries, he began searching for answers. But he didn't necessarily find answers about the problem—he found answers about his God. Daddy chose to run to God rather than running away from Him. He discovered the God of the Bible in a fresh way—as a loving God, a healing God, a restoring God, and, yes, as a God of miracles (see p. 213).

1. Describe a situation you face at the moment (or one you faced in the past) in which things just don't make sense. Did your trust in God come through it all or temporarily fall by the wayside?

_____

_____

_____

_____

_____

2. Write out the definitions for *delivering faith* and for *sustaining faith*. Then describe any experiences you've had that illustrate one or the other.

_____

_____

_____

_____

_____

_____

_____

> "When you face adversity, you need to remind yourself that whatever is trying to defeat you could very well be what God will use to promote you."
>
> *(p. 214)*

_____

_____

3. Even if you've already brought it up in previous questions, name your greatest adversity in life. Now ask yourself, "Could this be the very thing God will use to promote me?" Explain your answer.

_____

_____

_____

_____

_____

4. Imagine for a moment that your job was to defeat, resist, or hinder someone who lives out the statement: "For to me to live is Christ, and to die is gain" (Philippians 1:21).

- What could you do to scare or stop someone who doesn't live for himself and who considers death a real favor?
- How do you think the enemy feels about people who share Paul's radical, sold-out lifestyle in Christ?

- How do you think he feels about you (p. 214)?

_____

_____

_____

_____

_____

5. Would you pick a young, untested minister's son to pastor a church of thousands—even if he had never preached a single sermon in his life?

_____

_____

_____

_____

_____

I've described how God planted a deep urge or longing in my heart to pastor Lakewood Church after years of my avoiding every invitation to preach. It didn't make sense, but now it is clear that it was God.

6. Jot down some of the deep urges God has planted in your heart over the last year. What has He told you about these things? Do you believe you are to share with others what God has planted in you? Why or why not?

_____

_____

_____

_____

_____

7. You may know that I spent 17 years behind the scenes managing the TV production at Lakewood Church before I ever preached my first sermon. Have you (or someone else) convinced yourself that you are too old, too young, too

locked into old habits, or too afraid to do
anything different for God?

_____

_____

_____

_____

_____

_____

_____

_____

*"God has promised
that He will turn
your challenges into
stepping-stones for
promotion."*

(p. 217)

_____

8. What challenges in your life has God used as stepping-stones for promotion?
Write out your experience, then take a moment to give Him thanks for His
goodness to you.

_____

_____

_____

_____

_____

9. "Adversity often pushes us into our divine destiny" (p. 218). Describe an instance when adversity pushed you into your divine destiny. Read John 15. What
does God say about pruning and bearing fruit?

_____

_____

_____

_____

_____

CHAPTER 25

❧

THE JOY OF GIVING

WE WERE CREATED AND COMMANDED BY GOD TO *GIVE*. WE SHOULDN'T BE SURPRISED that God demonstrated supreme love in the most divine way—He *gave* (John 3:16). When we give in to our old nature, we demonstrate our selfishness in a carnal way—we *take*.

On the extreme end, some people *take* life as Cain did (Genesis 4:8). Others take another person's spouse, belongings, or livelihood.

1. Conduct an experiment to test my formula for depression and discouragement (p. 222). Think of a time when you were upset or worried or had lost your joy. Then answer the following questions:

   • What were you focused on during that difficult time?
   • Where was your emphasis?
   • What were you thinking about?

> "I [Paul] have shown you in every way, by laboring like this, that you must support the weak. And remember the words of the Lord Jesus, that He said, 'It is more blessed to give than to receive.' "
>
> *(Acts 20:35 NKJV, emphasis added)*

NOTE: Was your experience one of those instances when you were thinking about *your* problems? How did things turn out in that situation?

_____

_____

_____

_____

_____

2. Describe a time in your life when you followed the same advice I gave to the disgruntled and discouraged man who was living out of his car (pp. 222–223). How did you help others, and what happened in your life as a result?

_____

_____

_____

_____

_____

3. I've listed some ways to be a giver (pp. 223–224). Read the list below and briefly describe the acts of service you have done in the past. Explain how your own needs were met in the process. Then mark the items you would like to try in the future:

- Visit a nursing home or a children's hospital
- Call a friend and bring encouragement
- Help somebody else's child develop a relationship with God
- Help somebody financially who has less than you have
- Give someone a smile or a hug
- Mow somebody's lawn or bake them a cake
- Write someone an encouraging letter

_____

_____

_____

_____

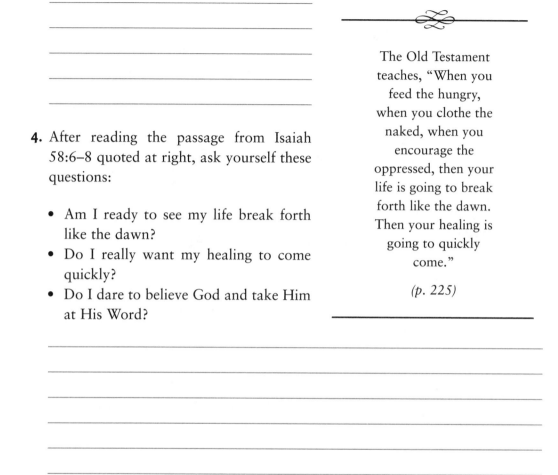

_____

_____

_____

_____

_____

4. After reading the passage from Isaiah 58:6–8 quoted at right, ask yourself these questions:

- Am I ready to see my life break forth like the dawn?
- Do I really want my healing to come quickly?
- Do I dare to believe God and take Him at His Word?

The Old Testament teaches, "When you feed the hungry, when you clothe the naked, when you encourage the oppressed, then your life is going to break forth like the dawn. Then your healing is going to quickly come."

(p. 225)

_____

_____

_____

_____

_____

5. On page 226, I shared my personal opinion about the link between miracles and selfless attitudes:

"I'm convinced that many people would receive the miracle they have been praying about if they would simply turn their attention away from themselves, away from their own needs and problems, and start to focus on being a blessing to other people."

Now tell me your opinion—do you think this is a true statement? Why or why not?

_____

_____

_____

_____

6. Do you know people who "live with their hands clenched"? Describe what you have observed about their lives, their priorities, and their quality of life. Does this describe you?

_____

_____

_____

_____

_____

A lot of people say, "God, when are You going to bless me?" But if we'd listen more carefully, maybe we'd hear God saying, "When are you going to start being a blessing?"

(p. 228)

7. What area of your life most needs a blessing right now? Think of ways you can start being a blessing in that area, and write it down. Set some realistic goals so you can follow through with this commitment.

_____

_____

_____

_____

8. Describe situations in your life in which you were given back whatever you gave. (I am not talking about "returned" gifts; I am referring to new blessings that came your way as a result of seed you sowed.)

_____

_____

_____

_____

_____

9. What if you had an abundance of wealth to share with others, like the young man from Saudi Arabia? How would you go about sharing your good fortune (p. 229)? Then write out some ways you can better develop a lifestyle of giving with the resources you have now.

_____

_____

_____

_____

Jesus said: "Inasmuch as you did it to one of the least of these My brethren, *you did it to Me*" (Matthew 25:40 NKJV, emphasis added). Too often, we read the statements of Jesus and unconsciously file them away as we would the casual statements of ordinary men.

10. Since Jesus always meant what He said, and since He always follows through on His promises, *how does that change your thinking* about giving, loving, and helping other people in need? Explain.

_____

_____

_____

_____

_____

_____

_____

"You have not lived today until you have done something for someone who cannot pay you back."

John Bunyan (p. 230)

_____

_____

_____

_____

Jesus Himself spelled this out even more clearly:

> "You have heard that it was said, 'You shall love your neighbor and hate your enemy.' But I say to you, love your enemies, bless those who curse you, do good to those who hate you, and pray for those who spitefully use you and persecute you, *that you may be sons of your Father in heaven . . .*" (Matthew 5:43–45, NKJV, emphasis added).

11. Does this passage sound more like a suggestion or a command? Why? Which of these have you observed, and which have you ignored?

_____

_____

_____

_____

_____

CHAPTER 26

SHOWING GOD'S KINDNESS AND MERCY

ARE YOU GOOD TO PEOPLE? THIS QUESTION IS EASY AS LONG AS YOU PICTURE YOUR friends and allies as the recipients of your kindness and generosity.

But things get uncomfortable when we are actually called to love our enemies. Are you good to people who dislike you; who insult or mistreat you in some way?

1. One Bible version says we should "aim to show kindness" and "seek to do good" to others (p. 231). These are action words; they are proactive, not passive. Describe some ways you aim and seek to do these things each day.

_____

_____

_____

_____

_____

_____

2. Early in this chapter, I described God's divine standards of conduct using phrases such as "God expects us to be bigger and better than that" (p. 231), and "God wants us to live by higher standards" (p. 232). It may not seem fair, and at times, it may even seem impossible! Read Philippians 2:13 and explain how this verse applies to your situation.

_____

_____

_____

_____

_____

Isaiah 55:9 says, "For as the heavens are higher than the earth, so are my ways higher than your ways, and my thoughts than your thoughts." This seems to be very apparent when we read, "Do not be overcome by evil, but overcome evil with good" (Romans 12:21 NKJV).

3. Explain in your own words why and how this verse differs from the way we often think evil should be handled.

_____

_____

_____

_____

_____

4. After reading my account of the cantankerous pizza lady (pp. 233–234), can you recall any situation in your life in which you were able to share God's kindness with someone in desperate need of it—even though you wanted to share something other than kindness with them?

_____

_____

_____

_____

Most of us reserve love for people who like us, respect us, and who generally return the same thing back to us. God's definition of love seems to be entirely different. The Bible says, "Love overlooks a person's faults . . . Anybody can return evil for evil, but God wants His people to help heal wounded hearts."

5. It has been said, "Hurt people hurt people." What might this say about some of the people who have hurt you? Does it help you understand why God wants you to help heal wounded hearts? Explain.

_____

_____

_____

_____

_____

The first roadblock to loving unlovely people may be labeled "My Grudge." As the Bible says, "Love doesn't hold a grudge. Love doesn't harbor unforgiveness" (p. 235).

6. Think of the most difficult person or painful memory currently troubling your life.

- Ask yourself: "Am I still holding a grudge against this person? Am I still harboring secret unforgiveness toward this individual because of the pain I feel?"
- If possible, share your answers to these questions with someone who cares. It must be someone who will pray with you to release all grudges, resentment, and unforgiveness. God's love will set you free!

_____

_____

_____

_____

_____

Corrie ten Boom was a Dutch survivor of the Nazi concentration and extermination camps during World War II. Her family was imprisoned for secretly harboring Jews. The family was split up, and the other members of Corrie's family died in those camps. Many years later, she encountered one of the former prison guards who had inflicted such pain on her family. She was able to forgive this man through the power of God's love.

7. Is there someone from the distant past in your life, or in the life of a loved one, who appears to be beyond any possibility of forgiveness or repentance?

   • Will you give that person to God by faith—along with everything they did to you, no matter how long ago it happened?
   • God's love knows no bounds, and His power can reach into the darkest of hearts—will you allow the miracle to begin in *your* heart?

   _____

   _____

   _____

   _____

   _____

Perhaps Paul said, "Don't grow weary in well doing" (p. 237), precisely because he knew we would grow weary in well doing! Some people just don't change very quickly. They may insult, abuse, or misuse you over and over again. It is for this kind of person, and this kind of difficult situation, that God says, "Don't wear out. Keep up the good work. When the time comes, you'll get a harvest!"

8. Think back to a situation in your life when you nearly quit, but managed to hold on until you finally experienced a turnaround and breakthrough.

   _____

   _____

   _____

   _____

_____

_____

_____

_____

_____

_____

_____

"God sees your acts
of kindness and
mercy . . ."

(p. 238)

9. Read Hebrews 6:10, and describe a time in your life when you enjoyed supernatural favor and blessings or unexpected promotion in your life. Was that time preceded by some difficult seasons of sowing? Explain.

_____

_____

_____

_____

_____

_____

_____

_____

_____

_____

CHAPTER 27

───────── ✦ ─────────

KEEP YOUR HEART OF COMPASSION OPEN

THE DAY MY DAD FOLLOWED THE COMPASSION IN HIS HEART AND GAVE MONEY TO A stranded young man in a Third World country, he was doing something very biblical (p. 239). The Bible says, "Cast thy bread upon the waters: for thou shalt find it after many days" (Ecclesiastes 11:1). The street version of Solomon's wise saying is, "What goes around comes around."

1. Do you really believe this principle? Have you ever applied it in your life? Have you ever been the beneficiary of good deeds sown by your parents or someone else? Explain.

_____

_____

_____

_____

_____

2. When have you been overwhelmed with a feeling of compassion? How did God use you to show someone you cared?

_____

_____

_____

_____

_____

_____

_____

_____

_____

_____

_____

~

"This world is
desperate to
experience the love
and compassion of
our God."

(p. 240)

3. The Bible is blunt at times. Scripture says, "If anyone sees his brother in need yet closes his heart of compassion, how can the love of God be in him?"

   • What is God saying you must do when you see a need?
   • What is implied if you don't do it?

_____

_____

_____

_____

_____

_____

4. Take the "Open Heart Test" right now (p. 241). Answer these questions and explain them as needed:

   • Are you concerned about other people, or are you concerned only about yourself?
   • Do you take time to make a difference, to encourage others, to lift their spirits, to make people feel better about themselves?
   • Do you follow the flow of love that God puts in your heart toward somebody in need?

- Are you mostly focused on your own plans? Are you willing to be interrupted and inconvenienced if it means you can help meet someone's need?

_____

_____

_____

_____

_____

_____

_____

_____

"But seek ye first the
kingdom of God,
and his
righteousness; and
all these things
[food, drink,
clothing] shall be
added unto you."

(Matthew 6:33)

On page 243, we read the promise Jesus made to each of us: "Take my word for this: If you will focus on meeting other people's needs, God will always make sure your needs are supplied. God will take care of your problems for you" (see Matthew 6:33). His promise is far more powerful than my words. The Scripture passages we've already studied in this book describe what goes on in God's Kingdom and why.

5. Are you ready to seek first the Kingdom and His righteousness and trust Him for your needs? How does this relate to our need to "be on the lookout for people we can bless" (p. 242)?

_____

_____

_____

_____

_____

6. "Sometimes if we would just take the time to listen to people, we could help initiate a healing process in their lives" (pp. 242–243). Reflect on instances in your

life when someone took the time to listen to you and helped initiate a healing process in your life.

_____

_____

_____

_____

_____

7. Do you believe that you need to care, even when you don't know all the answers? Why (p. 243)?

_____

_____

_____

_____

_____

_____

_____

_____

"For as many as are led by the Spirit of God, these are [children] of God."

(Romans 8:14 NKJV)

8. How does this Scriptural truth apply to divine appointments where God arranges for you to bump into someone who is about to make a wrong decision, or who is crying out for His help in a terrible situation? Explain, and give examples if you have already seen this happen in your life.

_____

_____

_____

_____

_____

9. Are you prepared to be God's answer to someone's desperate and lonely prayer (p. 245)? Has your heart of compassion already led you into situations where you risked appearing silly or foolish in an attempt to bring hope to someone else (p. 246)? What did you learn from the experience?

_____

_____

_____

_____

_____

_____

10. Describe a situation in which you sensed a deep compassion for a family member or friend (what the world might call a "premonition"), but failed to act on it, only to discover your heart was actually very accurate (p. 247).

_____

_____

_____

_____

_____

_____

11. God blessed me with the opportunity to show supernatural love to my daddy before he died (pp. 247–249). How does this story compel you to keep your heart of compassion open to God's lead?

_____

_____

_____

_____

_____

_____

CHAPTER 28

THE SEED MUST LEAD

SEEDTIME AND HARVEST, THE LAW OF SOWING AND REAPING; THIS ETERNAL PRINCIPLE saturates every part of our life on earth. Unfortunately, you wouldn't know it from the way we live!

Perhaps it is because so many people in Western industrialized nations have left the farm and forgotten the earthy wisdom of the soil. On the other hand, even the computer generation understands that if you feed (sow) garbage into a computer in the form of flawed programming, then you will get (reap) garbage out.

There is no confusion here about "Which comes first—the chicken or the egg?" The seed must lead (p. 250). First you sow; then, and only then, can you reap.

"Do not be deceived, God is not mocked; for whatever a man sows, that he will also reap."

(Galatians 6:7 NKJV)

1. List some of the needs in your life, including needs in your family, church, and community. Now create another list of possible "seeds" you could sow by faith to reap a harvest in those areas.

_____

_____

_____

_____

2. Review the featured message about Isaac on page 251 called "Famine in the Land." Did you notice something odd about Isaac's great harvest? He sowed seed in the middle of a great famine! It may fly in the face of human logic, but your greatest planting season usually comes in the middle of your greatest need. Describe some of the desperate planting seasons in your life and what you reaped from the seeds you sowed in those seasons.

_____

_____

_____

_____

_____

_____

Genuine faith is always working faith. Paul wrote many of our New Testament teachings on faith, yet he willingly worked with his hands and labored constantly to bring the good news to hurting people. This is how the seed leads: FIRST, you trust in the Lord. SECOND, you go out and do something good (p. 251).

3. Identify a time when you or someone you know failed to do one or the other. Explain what consequences followed.

_____

_____

_____

_____

_____

_____

4. What does it mean in your life for you to be "more seed-oriented than need-oriented" (p. 252)? Give some practical examples.

_____

_____

_____

_____

_____

5. When Daddy needed thousands of dollars to launch the first building program for the church, he understood that "one of the best things he could do in that time of famine was to plant some seed" (p. 252). Is there a famine in your life or ministry? Explain how you plan to "sow a seed in the time of need."

_____

_____

_____

_____

_____

6. Use practical examples from your life to demonstrate the meaning of the Scripture that says in part: "By watering others, he waters himself" (p. 252).

_____

_____

_____

_____

_____

_____

_____

_____

> "If you will focus on giving generously to others, God will make sure your own life is refreshed, even if you must go through a dry, dreary wilderness."
>
> *(pp. 252–253)*

Daniel Kelley suffered the sorrow of losing his beloved wife, but then he began sowing seeds of comfort at funerals for people he didn't even know (pp. 252–253).

133

Job suffered from the false comfort of his friends during his trial of adversity—but in a similar way, the first thing Job did toward the end was to plant seed by praying for his friends:

> "And the Lord restored Job's losses *when he prayed for his friends.* Indeed the Lord gave Job twice as much as he had before" (Job 42:10 NKJV, emphasis added).

7. Has God planted a gift in you through adversity that may help others in need? What are you doing to plant this new seed into the lives of others?

_____

_____

_____

_____

_____

_____

_____

8. On page 254, I said: "Learn to stretch your faith . . . If you want an extraordinary harvest, sow an extraordinary seed." What does this mean to you, and how do you intend to apply it in your life?

_____

_____

_____

_____

_____

_____

9. Do you sow a little or a lot (p. 255)? Are you a generous sower or a cautious sower? Why?

_____

_____

_____

_____

_____

10. What teachings have you heard on tithes and offerings? Did this chapter teach something different than what you believe to be true? How has your perspective on tithing and offerings changed after reading pages 256–257?

_____

_____

_____

_____

_____

_____

_____

_____

_____

_____

_____

> "The Scripture is not ambiguous about this matter. It says, 'In everything you do, put God first, and he will direct you and crown your efforts with success.'
>
> *(p. 257)*

I am convinced that God gets excited when He delivers such powerful promises to His people. The area of our finances is the only instance where God challenges us to prove Him. Are you up to the challenge?

CHAPTER 29

SOWING AND GROWING

GOD'S WORD IS FILLED WITH WORD PICTURES. JESUS SKILLFULLY MADE DIVINE TRUTH come alive in the minds of His hearers using descriptive word pictures—living snapshots taken from the field, the stream, the average home, and from visual landmarks.

Nothing speaks of stagnancy and lifelessness as well as the Dead Sea. It represents the ultimate "Hoarder's Heaven" filled with one of the world's richest deposits of accumulated minerals and salts. Yet, in its natural form, the sea is perfectly useless because of its one-way flow. A lot comes in but nothing goes out.

1. If someone were to describe your life with word pictures, what images would come to mind?

- Do you give as much as you receive? Are you a rolling, sparkling mountain stream filled with purified, crystal-clear water bringing refreshment and life everywhere you flow (see John 7:38–39)?
- Or, is your life framed in the image and likeness of the Dead Sea; marked by a one-way flow of wealth and nutrients in a sluggish current lost in a stagnant and stinking life pool that only receives, holds, and hoards?

_____

_____

2. The fundamental principle applies in every area of life: "You must sow the seed first, then you will reap a harvest" (p. 259). Even God Himself is committed to following the divine pattern He established. He wanted many sons and daughters so *first* He sowed His only Son (Hebrews 2:10, Romans 8:29).

- Is this principle at work in your life?
- In what areas are you first sowing good seed for a good harvest later?
- In what areas are you going backwards? You can recognize these areas by the type of if/then and when/then excuses they produce: "When I get out of this problem, then I'll help out someone else. Just leave me alone right now."

_____

_____

_____

_____

_____

_____

"God's supernatural power seems to be activated by unselfish gestures."

(p. 259)

_____

_____

3. When you have a problem—whether it concerns your job, your marriage, your finances, or your children—do you generally concentrate on your need or do you think about what kind of seed you can sow into that problem?

_____

_____

_____

_____

_____

_____

4. What would you do if you were in deep poverty and deep trouble? (You may be facing this very situation!) Honestly describe how you would probably respond to this kind of crisis and why.

_____

_____

_____

_____

_____

Compare your response with what the early Christians did in Corinth when they faced deep poverty and trouble: "In the midst of their great trouble, they stayed full of joy and they gave generously to others" (p. 259).

5. Describe God's principle designed to supply our needs during life's tough times (p. 260). Have you applied this principle in your life? Why or why not?

_____

_____

_____

_____

_____

6. Read my account of the miraculous way a total stranger helped us when we were stranded in India, a few years after Daddy helped the stranded traveler in a foreign airport (pp. 261–262). Do you remember ways in which seeds you sowed years ago have produced harvests in your life recently? Did you sow any good seeds in recent years?

_____

_____

_____
_____
_____
_____
_____
_____
_____
_____
_____
_____

> "For God is not
> unjust to forget *your*
> *work and labor of*
> *love* [seeds] which
> you have shown
> [sown] toward His
> name, in that you
> have ministered to
> the saints, and do
> minister."
>
> *(Hebrews 6:10 NKJV,*
> *emphasis added)*

7. Think of the times you've quietly and secretly sown time, money, encouragement, resources, and prayer into the lives of people around you and in your church. God never forgets good seed sown.

_____
_____
_____
_____
_____

8. Give examples of ways you look for, seek out, and aim for fresh opportunities to sow good seed into another person's need—especially those situations when no one but God knows. His rewards are far greater than the best man can offer!

_____
_____
_____

_____

_____

_____

_____

"Don't let anyone
convince you that it
doesn't make a
difference to give."

(p. 264)

It appears that God is especially generous to especially generous people, but divine generosity has nothing to do with the amount of a gift. He regards the generosity of the gift and the spirit and motive behind it. Cornelius "was chosen . . . because of his giving spirit" (p. 264). Jesus praised the poor widow who gave a total of one penny because ". . . she *out of her poverty* put in *all that she had,* her *whole livelihood*" (Mark 12:44b NKJV, emphasis added).

9. Do you think God will choose to send special blessings to you because of your giving spirit? Explain.

_____

_____

_____

_____

10. We *know* that Cornelius prayed because the Scriptures say he "prayed often" (p. 264). We may also safely assume that the widow Jesus mentioned prayed as well. However, they both added action to their prayers in the form of sowing seed. How can you make a difference by sowing a seed?

_____

_____

_____

_____

_____

CHAPTER 30

❦

HAPPINESS IS A CHOICE

SOME PEOPLE GO THROUGH LIFE CONSTANTLY DEMANDING THEIR RIGHTS. ONE OF THE strangest rights we claim is the right to be sour and negative. "Hey, I was born this way, I've always been this way, and I will always be this way. Now leave me alone."

Much of our comedy is focused around people who respond to life's hard situations with cynical, biting comments about others and themselves. One of the milder jokes along this line goes, "If I didn't have bad luck, I would have no luck at all!"

John, the apostle who received the Revelation of Jesus Christ in his final years of life, declared to Christians in the early church, "Greater is he that is in you, than he that is in the world" (1 John 4:4b).

> ❦
>
> "I am come that they might have life, and that they might have it more abundantly."
>
> *(John 10:10 NKJV)*

Your faith doesn't rest on the foundation of some dusty collection of religious do's and don'ts. God Himself lives and works inside you! That fact, alone, is enough to transform the way you approach each day of life. Make the switch *today* with a clear choice: "I choose to be happy!"

1. Can you identify any benefits from being unhappy? Which do you think is more difficult for you, living with a positive outlook or a negative one?

_____

_____

_____

_____

_____

_____

_____

2. The Bible says, "Therefore do not worry about tomorrow, for tomorrow will worry about its own things. Sufficient for the day is its own trouble" (Matthew 6:34 NKJV). Think about a time in your life when worry and concern over the unknown future nearly destroyed your ability to enjoy God's blessings in the present.

_____

_____

_____

"Happiness is a
decision you make,
not an emotion you
feel."

(p. 270)

_____

_____

_____

Did something inside you bristle or resist this statement about happiness? Perhaps you and I have been influenced by society and culture more than we know. The idea is widely promoted and believed that happiness is strictly an emotion, a state of life seen on the silver screen that can easily be purchased on the layaway plan or by credit card.

Peace is an important component of happiness. Consider what the Bible says about peace:

Jesus said:
"Peace I leave with you, My peace I give to you; not as the world gives do I give to you. Let not your heart be troubled, neither let it be afraid" (John 14:27 NKJV).

Paul said:
"Be anxious for nothing, but in everything by prayer and supplication, with thanksgiving, let your requests be made known to God; and the peace of God, which surpasses all understanding, will guard your hearts and minds through Christ Jesus" (Philippians 4:6–7 NKJV).

3. In the light of these Scriptures, why should we never allow circumstances to dictate our decisions, steal our peace, quench our thanksgiving, or trouble our hearts?

_____

_____

_____

_____

_____

Solomon warned that it is "the little foxes that spoil the tender vines" (see Song of Solomon 2:15). The little irritating things in our lives often have incredible power to spoil our lives. Why? It is because *we give them power* through our choices.

4. When have you allowed little things—such as toys in the driveway, that maddening squeak in the car, the insulting honk on the freeway, or the whistle in the air vent at work—to steal your peace, ruin your evening, or spoil an entire day for your family or coworkers?

_____

_____

_____

_____

_____

The truth is that no matter what happens in life, you may choose how you will respond to circumstances. "God said He would never let us go through something that is too difficult for us to handle. If your desire is great enough, you can stay calm and cool no matter what comes against you in life" (p. 271).

5. Do you believe the statement above deep inside, where it really counts? Describe a time in your life when you experienced peace in the middle of a storm. If it hasn't happened yet in your life, then share a situation in which things went wrong, and imagine how things might have been different if this truth had been applied.

_____

_____

_____

_____

_____

_____

6. David the Psalmist set a "gold standard" for daily victory in the face of problems. He said, "This is the day the Lord has made. I will rejoice and be glad in it" (see p. 272). He kept his focus on *today*, and he made a decision and a declaration about how he would respond and interact with his day.

- If you are waiting on God, understand that He owns time. He is waiting on you! Positive change begins with right choices. What right choices can you make today?
- How will you apply David's biblical standard for daily living to your life, right now?

_____

_____

_____

_____

_____

7. Explain why big events will not keep you happy, and why it doesn't pay to suspend happiness while waiting for your problems to be solved.

_____

_____

_____

_____

_____

_____

8. Do you smile very often? Do you restrict your smile-time to ice cream times—those seasons when life seems sweet and creamy (p. 278)? In contrast, explain Paul's approach to contentment (see Philippians 4:11), and how you plan to apply the same principles in your own life.

_____

_____

_____

_____

_____

_____

_____

_____

CHAPTER 31

BEING A PERSON OF EXCELLENCE

DO YOU LIVE TO GET BY, TO GET AHEAD, OR TO PLEASE GOD? THESE THREE CHOICES ARE totally incompatible. Only *one* choice is acceptable to God.

1. If you want to live your best life now, how do you overcome a past track record littered with the debris of *just get by* performances and self-centered *get ahead* choices and catastrophes? Discuss practical ways you might do this in your life (pp. 282–283).

"God doesn't bless mediocrity. He blesses excellence. The Scripture says, 'Whatever you do, work at it with your whole heart, not unto men, but do it unto God knowing that God will reward you.'"

(p. 282)

2. Remember that in every area of life, it is God's opinion that counts. He sees everything, and nothing is hidden from Him. The principle is simple: Take care of what God has given to you or assigned to your keeping. Then He will entrust you with more (p. 283). How does this principle affect your choices concerning:

- When you begin work and when you go home.
- How you discipline your time usage and work ethic each day.
- How you communicate and deal with people on the job, in your home, and in the community.
- How you reflect God's excellence in your personal appearance and language, and even how you care for the appearance of your home, lawn, automobiles, and desk.
- What you do and do not report and claim on your tax forms.
- How you keep your promises—*every* promise you make in public or in private.

_____

_____

_____

_____

_____

3. "Subtle compromises of integrity will keep you from God's best" (pp. 285–286). Review the examples of compromise given in this chapter and honestly audit your decisions over the last month or year.

- Where have you made compromises that you now realize are limiting you or keeping you from God's best for your life?
- What will you do about them?

_____

_____

_____

_____

_____

4. Paul the apostle couldn't have been any clearer when he warned us: "All who desire to live godly in Christ Jesus will suffer persecution" (2 Timothy 3:12b NKJV).

- Are you willing to pay the price to do the right thing (pp. 288–290)?
- Describe instances in which you did have to pay a price to do the right thing instead of the politically correct or less painful thing.
- Describe a situation in which you did not pass the test, but learned from the experience.

_____

_____

_____

_____

_____

As you read the story of the builder who secretly cut corners to squeeze more profit from a house, only to discover he was cheating on his own house—did you realize that God says you and I are literally building our own houses with our life choices (pp. 291–292)?

Whether we realize it or not, we all are building our own homes. Do you remember what Jesus said about the two men who built houses upon the foundations of their choices (Matthew 7:24–27)?

The wise man *chooses* to build on a rock foundation by obeying and living by God's Word, regardless of the difficulties involved. He experiences temporary hardship but enjoys eternal stability that can withstand any storm.

The foolish man builds on the ever-shifting sand of politically correct, man-pleasing choices while dismissing God's Word as too difficult. He may enjoy a brief period of easy living, but total catastrophe inevitably follows when the storms of life arise.

5. Based on your choice of foundations, what kind of person are you? Describe the "house" you have built with your choices.

_____

_____

_____

_____

_____

Do you realize who your real Boss is (p. 294)? The Bible tells us that promotion comes from the Lord, as does the power to get wealth (Psalm 75:6, Deuteronomy 8:18). However, surface appearances can lull us into complacency.

We tend to think to ourselves, "Well, God's name isn't on the checks I get every month." No, but His name is written on our hearts, and if we bring shame to His name through our ungodly choices, we will be held personally accountable. God is your Boss, and He keeps the only records that count for eternity!

6. Identify any areas in your work habits or standards of excellence that need to be "upgraded" to a higher level to match God's gold standard of integrity. Outline how and when you plan to make it happen.

_____

_____

_____

_____

_____

7. As I explained at the end of chapter 31, I discovered in a very personal way just how important it is to build "another man's house" *as if* it were your own. I had no idea as I worked to remodel the television platform that Daddy would be promoted to heaven, leaving *me* to fill the spot behind the podium!

   • How are you building the "house" God placed in your life?
   • Has God planted you in another person's life, business, or ministry for a reason? How are you helping to build that "home"?

_____

_____

_____

_____

CHAPTER 32

———— ❧ ————

LIVING WITH ENTHUSIASM

THE ONLY WAY TO LIVE *YOUR BEST LIFE NOW* IS TO LIVE THE LIFE GOD HAS GIVEN YOU with enthusiasm and excitement. In fact, since God lives in your heart, you should be one of the happiest people on earth!

People should notice something different about you wherever you go—even without the outward assistance of Christian T-shirts, logos, super-sized Bibles, slogans, and bumper stickers. There is nothing wrong with these things, but "the proof is in the pudding, not in the container."

I've heard it said that one reason so many people show no interest in what the church has to offer is that so many saints look as if they have been "baptized in pickle juice"!

1. Have you lost your fire, your passion, and your enthusiasm for the Lord and His Kingdom?

_____

_____

_____

_____

_____

_____

Jesus sternly warned the Church:

"Nevertheless I have this against you, that *you have left your first love*. Remember therefore from where you have fallen; repent and do the first works, or else I will come to you quickly and remove your lampstand from its place; unless you repent" (Revelation 2:4–5 NKJV, emphasis added).

The Lord gives us a three-step "love recovery plan" to relight our fires and reestablish our lost zeal:

- Remember therefore from where you have fallen.
- Repent.
- Do the first works.

2. Why do you think Christians must constantly return to these three fundamental steps of enthusiastic Christ-centered living?

_____

_____

_____

_____

_____

_____

Do you drink something each day, or do you save up your thirst for your weekly drink of water on Sunday afternoon? That is ridiculous, I know, but it sounds a lot like the way we handle our relationship with God.

John said in the Book of Revelation, "And he showed me a pure river of water of life, clear as crystal, proceeding out of the throne of God and of the Lamb" (Revelation 22:1). You and I were created to *drink* from that pure water of life every day and every moment for eternity!

3. Have you been saving up your thirst for God for your weekly drink at Sunday service? No wonder you feel dry, weak, and listless in your spirit. You are

nearly dead from spiritual dehydration! Jesus still promised, "He who believes in Me, as the Scripture has said, out of his heart will flow rivers of living water" (John 7:37b–38 NKJV). If you feel dry and weak spiritually, determine your next steps toward restoration!

_____

_____

_____

_____

_____

_____

_____

4. We are supernatural, eternal beings who live temporarily in an earthbound natural environment filled with distractions and frustration. We can become stagnant if we are not careful (p. 297). Examine your life for any evidence that life's routine may have lulled you to sleep, or distracted, frustrated, or hindered your progress in Christ.

_____

_____

_____

_____

_____

_____

_____

5. Some Christians just don't like to hear the word _enthusiasm_ used in church settings. They feel it is almost an "unspiritual" word. The truth would set them free if they allowed it to—enthusiasm literally stems from two Greek words meaning "inspired by God" (p. 297). Are you enthusiastic about your life in God? Why or why not?

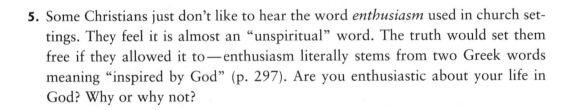

_____

_____
_____
_____

6. As I mentioned in this final chapter, things may not be perfect in your life, but it doesn't let you off of God's hook. "Never lag in zeal, but be aglow and on fire, serving the Lord enthusiastically" (Romans 12:11). Take the Bible zeal test (and explain your answers):

- Do you lag in zeal?
- Are you aglow and on fire?
- Do you serve the Lord enthusiastically, inspired by God? If not, then _why not_? If so, then keep going farther!

_____
_____
_____
_____
_____
_____

When we talk about zeal, we cannot limit it to getting excited during a church worship service (although there is nothing wrong with that). Wherever you are in life, make the most of it and be the best that you can be (p. 298). Be enthusiastic in everything you do, give it everything you have. Get so hot in your zeal that you become contagious!

7. What are you spreading with your life? Boredom or enthusiasm? Cynicism or eternal hope? Funeral-like depression or marriage-party excitement and expectation?

_____
_____

For some reason, most people regard enthusiasm as an abnormal state in normal life. Oddly enough, enthusiasm is a highly regarded requirement among bosses, businesses, and industries dependent on a steady supply of high-quality, highly motivated leaders. Most important of all, God, the Lord of all, wants us to live with zeal and enthusiasm.

"This could be the day . . ." (pp. 301–303). If you start each day with enthusiasm about God and His unlimited possibilities, you can't help but expect to encounter God's blessings! No matter how dark the day may appear, say to yourself and anyone else who is near:

- "This could be the day my dream comes true because my God is ever faithful!"
- "This could be the day of my deliverance and the beginning of the greatest turnaround of my life!"
- "God is on the throne and I am seated with Him. All things are possible *because I believe*!"
- "This could be the day things turn around because I'm *living my best life now*!"